En

MW00773006

In *Fierce & Free,* Kelly Master calls to our core... It's the call to step out of your tethers and discover the "wild." It's our Spirit DNA! We are created to launch, pioneer, soar, and ride the storm. Kelly not only calls but also shows the way to discover, believe, and embrace the TRUE of you. As you read and see yourself in the pages of this book, you will also see your path to the "more" that is *your* glorious, untamed future... the path to live *Fierce & Free.*

—Dr. Michelle Burkett,
Director of Patricia King's
Women in Ministry Network,
Michelle Burkett Ministries

Kelly Master's passion to see women set free and walk in their God-given freedom is the core message of this book. She shares deeply, honestly, and with vulnerability about details of her life that most people would rather not touch and therefore remain unhealed. In doing this, Kelly shows powerfully how God's purposes for us can be achieved as we step out in faith and believe God for the impossible.

—Kemi Koleoso, Founder of Courage Women's Conference, Speaker and Pastor at Jubilee Church London, UK

In *Fierce & Free*, Kelly Master speaks to the soul of women in a way that will set a burning fire to fulfill life's dreams and divine purpose. Kelly provides practical steps for women of all ages to explore, acknowledge, accept, and engage in effectuating God's call on their lives. This masterpiece is an empowering short read full of wisdom, compassion, and biblical truths that will encourage women to excel beyond complacency into a sphere of procurement. As a pastor and psychotherapist, I can't wait to share this monumental work with my congregants and clients.

—Dr. Tiffany Gilmore, LCSW, M.DIV

Definitely one of the most inspiring books I have read. The author used her own stories of brokenness to show how a loving Father can take the very things meant to destroy us and turn it into a story of forgiveness, redemption, and hope! This book will be a must-have in our counseling

center so we can encourage other women with this beau-
tifully written example of God's grace, mercy, and love!

—Andrea Hennessee,
Founder and Pastoral Counselor Life Focus Center

Fierce & Free will ignite your potential and accelerate your
heart's desire for more! Passionate, fiery, and anointed
Kelly Master shares her story of transformation from
dysfunction, pain, and addiction, to a victorious life only
possible through the cross of Christ Jesus! The praise
song, "Look What the Lord has Done," epitomizes Kelly's
story! Let this book awaken and empower you to pursue
your purpose and destiny. It's time to take all limits off!
It's time to be *Fierce & Free*!!

—Rev., Dr. Jamie Morgan,
Mentor to Women in Ministry,
Trailblazer Mentorship Network

Wow. Just wow. Real, raw, and vulnerable! Kelly so
honestly shares her story while encouraging all of us to
fly from our cages and experience true freedom through
Christ. I especially love the, "action points" at the end of

each chapter. This book provides a very real opportunity for you to experience personal change."

—Joanne Sharp,
Founder of EncouragHER

Fierce & Free is a clarion call for women to rise and embrace their full potential without excuse. Kelly Master's passion and faith are contagious, and each chapter will invoke you to break free from all limitations and live with greater purpose, joy, and passion.

—Deedra Determan, Business Coach,
Host of the DO IT MY WAY Podcast,
Founder of D2 Branding

Bravo! Kelly Master combines riveting life stories with inspiration and motivation in the book, Fierce & Free. I couldn't put it down. From the first chapter, through her tough life, all the way to the miracle ending, she's got your attention. The Action Steps at the end of each chapter move the story from hers to yours, bringing home the lessons learned. If you're ready to "ignite your potential," read this book!

—Marnie Swedberg, International Leadership Mentor

This is a powerful, life-altering book that you hold in your hands. Kelly shares her life story with complete openness and honesty. It will bring you to tears, and you will identify with parts of her story, as no one is exempt from pain and trauma. The highlight though is the very real, undeniable love of our Heavenly Father who persistently pursues each one of us. Read this slowly, allowing its truths to sink in, and thoughtfully answer the questions at the end of each chapter. You can't help but find incredible freedom and wholeness on the other side.

—Joanne Eisenhart,
Founding Pastor True North Church NJ

No matter where you are in life, as you read these inspiring words from Kelly Master, you will hear the unmistakable call to freedom. I encourage you to allow the powerful message in "Fierce and Free" to lead you to boldly lay hold of your destiny.

—Patti White,
Founder Executive Director
New Beginnings Women's Center

God has truly anointed Kelly! Her insights are life-changing, and her enthusiasm is infectious. "A must-read book!"

—Teresa Richenberger,
Founder of Rahab's Retreat & Ranch

You were born to WIN! You are a WINNER! You are reading this right now because God has a calling on your life and He wants you to WIN! Through *Fierce & Free,* Kelly shows you how to do exactly that, WIN! This is a must-read if you are truly ready to tap into your fullest potential, become who God created you to be, and live a life of purpose and impact! Kelly's powerful story along with her unmatched wisdom, will inspire, motivate, and empower you to live a life of freedom! This brilliant book is way more than just a book; it is a roadmap, inspired by God, on exactly what you can do to take your life to the next level, how to ignite your potential, to live FIERCE so that you can live a life of freedom! Read it! Do what Kelly says to do, and you will WIN! Go WIN WINNER!

—Jonathan Conneely, "Coach JC" Performance coach,
motivational speaker, author, entrepreneur,
and founder of the Win All Day movement

It's not every day that we find a joyful and tenacious leader willing to be completely open about the abuse and brokenness that they experienced early in their lives. Each chapter of this powerful book has its own unique healing opportunity for women (and men) of any age. I highly recommend it not only for those that come from a background of addiction and abuse but also for those who are yet to break free from the prisons of wrong mindsets.

—Jessica Romero, Missionary,
Evangelist & Trainer - FIRE International

I read this book in one breath! Kelly's words immediately absorbed me, and I lost track of time. My heart breaks for the past experiences she's had to endure but is joyful and grateful for the amazing woman she has become in Christ and for the divine difference Kelly makes in the lives of others. May the Lord bless Kelly endlessly on this amazing journey of delivering His Word and bringing hope and guidance to those who are searching for His love, strength, and protection.

—Miranda Coppoolse,
Behavioral Analyst & Forensic Interviewer

FIERCE & free

Ignite *your* Potential

KELLY MASTER

FREILING
PUBLISHING

Copyright © 2023 by Kelly Master
First Paperback Edition

All rights reserved. No part of this publication may be reproduced, distributed, or transmitted in any form or by any means, including photocopying, recording, or other electronic or mechanical methods, without the prior written permission of the publisher, except in the case of brief quotations embodied in critical reviews and certain other noncommercial uses permitted by copyright law.
For permission requests, write to the publisher, addressed "Attention: Permissions Coordinator," at the address below.

Some names, businesses, places, events, locales, incidents, and identifying details inside this book have been changed to protect the privacy of individuals.

Bible versions used:

Scripture taken from the New King James Version® (NKJV). Copyright © 1982 by Thomas Nelson. Used by permission. All rights reserved.

Tree of Life (TLV) Translation of the Bible. Copyright © 2015 by The Messianic Jewish Family Bible Society.

The Holy Bible, English Standard Version (ESV). ESV® Text Edition: 2016. Copyright © 2001 by Crossway Bibles, a publishing ministry of Good News Publishers.

Scripture quotations marked TPT are from The Passion Translation®. Copyright © 2017, 2018, 2020 by Passion & Fire Ministries, Inc. Used by permission. All rights reserved. ThePassionTranslation.com.

The Message (MSG). Copyright © 1993, 2002, 2018 by Eugene H. Peterson.

Photo credit: Bokeh Love Photography

Published by Freiling Publishing, a division of Freiling Agency, LLC.

P.O. Box 1264
Warrenton, VA 20188

www.FreilingPublishing.com

PB ISBN: 978-1-956267-99-0
eBook ISBN: 979-8-9874834-0-4

Printed in the United States of America

Contents

Acknowledgments

WRITING THIS BOOK was quite a journey, and I want to acknowledge a few key people who helped me accomplish the task.

To my husband, Michael, I honor you and thank God for your persistence, honesty, and belief in me to write Fierce and Free. You had the vision to see the impact and the courage to push me to completion. Thank you for embracing God's call on my life.

To my children, I write for you and the generations to follow. You are deeply cherished. I pray that you live fierce and free, embracing all the Lord has for you. I love you.

To my Editor, Christen Jeschke, thank you for believing in me. Your encouragement, patience, and ability to provoke me to deeper places in my heart helped me release my authentic voice.

Toyin, thank you for relentlessly pursuing and believing in me to tell my story.

Coach JC and Deedra, thank you for igniting an unstoppable flame inside my heart.

I owe a special thank you to Irene, Joan, Peg, Tammy, Cass, Jodi, and everyone who has prayed and encouraged me to walk in my calling. Your prayers gave wind to my wings.

Living Fierce and Free,
Kelly Master

Introduction

IT IS TIME. My sister, are you ready to embark on an exciting adventure? Consider this book your invitation to the journey. *Fierce and Free* is a community of Christian women who believe in the power of the Holy Spirit and are ready to see their lives transformed. We are women strengthened by battle scars carrying dreams unrealized, poised to emerge from the shadow of our limitations. Join the *Fierce and Free* movement today.

Did you once have grand dreams for your life and are discouraged that these dreams remain unfulfilled? Does it feel as if God's promises have been dormant in your heart and will never come to pass? Have you given up believing in your heart's desires because you feel your dreams have died? If that is the case, you are perfectly positioned for a God-sized miracle. Without death, there is no resurrection. This is your time to see the manifested promises of God fulfilled in your life. He is faithful, and He does not lie. The Word of God states, *"So shall My word be that goes forth from My mouth; it shall not return to Me void, but it shall accomplish what I please, and it shall prosper in the thing for which I sent it"* (Isaiah 55:11 NKJV).

It's time to dust off your sword and pick it up with authority—to wage war again for the prophetic promises over your life.

There is no coincidence you are holding this book in your hand today. God Almighty, the maker of heaven and earth, who knit you together in your mother's womb, created you purposefully. In this world of eight billion people, nobody can accomplish the plans designed explicitly for you. You are unique and one of a kind. You have gifts and callings that the world needs. Stop shrinking back, my sister, and rise in confidence that our God who called you has equipped you and desires that you walk in your full potential.

What sets your heart on fire? Let's intentionally remove the clutter and pinpoint your heart's passions so you can SOAR to new heights, blaze new trails, and create your most significant impact. Within you is the DNA of God. You are fearfully and wonderfully made in His image, and all things are possible. You are a world changer and history maker. Who told you that you are not enough? They lied. Stop sitting on the sidelines. Stop listening to the excuses. This is your time, and you are more than able.

I have written this book for such a time as this. On this journey, I will help you.

- Discover your God-given PURPOSE
- Activate the promises of God in your life
- Break through cycles of defeat
- Create and conquer new goals
- Operate from a higher perspective
- Increase your faith and believe in God for the impossible

Sister, stop waiting for someone else's permission to shine. Give yourself permission to soar and lay hold of everything God has for you.

Not that I have already obtained this or been perfected,
but I press on if only I might take hold of that for which
Messiah Yeshua took hold of me.
(Philippians 3:12 TLV)

1

A Call to Soar

But they who wait for the Lord shall renew their strength;
they shall mount up with wings like eagles; they shall run
and not be weary; they shall walk and not faint.
(Isaiah 40:31 ESV)

EAGLES ENTRANCE ME. They are majestic creatures
that spread their wings and effortlessly soar through
the vast open skies, swooping and rising in an intricate
dance of grace and power. They are fierce, strong-winged
warriors whose claws maintain a gripping force that is
ten times greater than the grip of humans. An eagle's
impeccable vision allows it to see its prey up to two miles
away. It is an incredible species.

Unlike other birds, eagles have a fascinating ability
to rise above raging storms. While other birds attempt
to flee the oncoming disturbance, the eagle flies directly
into it, embracing the turbulence to soar high above the
wind-whipped chaos.

I once heard a story of a wounded eagle that a group of volunteers had discovered and nursed back to health. They tended to the eagle's injuries and nurtured it until it was ready to fly. The eagle was strengthened and prepared to return to its natural habitat. Excited volunteers carried the large cage to an open field, and curious spectators gathered to capture the moment.

The volunteers released the cage door with great fanfare while everyone watched with rapt anticipation. Eager onlookers waited expectantly, hoping to catch a glimpse of the eagle flying through the open cage door before soaring skyward. The eagle didn't move.

The shocked crowd stood stunned as they waited for the eagle to budge. Awkward moments stretched into minutes as the onlookers began to chatter, expressing their doubts that the bird would ever leave the comfort of its cage or dare to fly again. *Maybe the eagle had been held captive too long? Perhaps freedom was no longer an option for this once majestic bird.*

As more time passed, the crowd began dissipating, believing that the eagle would never be free. Doubt had taken hold, declaring that freedom wasn't an option for this bird and that the sanctuary must become its permanent home.

The curious staff approached the cage, deliberating whether to return the eagle to the sanctuary or give it more time. As they debated, they were stunned by the appearance of another eagle. Overhead, high above the crowd, a magnificent eagle soared through the beautiful skies. The eagle in flight released a series of powerful calls that pierced the chatter below and beckoned to the caged eagle.

Hearing the calls, the caged eagle responded as one who remembered her identity and capability. The once-captive eagle stretched out her wings and flew! She soared and dipped high above the spectators as she celebrated in a flight of freedom.

Something powerful happens when one who lives in freedom releases a call to another in captivity. If you are honest, you may relate to the caged eagle. Perhaps you were injured and lived in imprisonment, but captivity does not have the final say. The cage is not your home!

Today, I release a clarion call over your life. You have wings to fly; lift your vision higher and soar to new heights! Open your spiritual ears, lean into heaven, and hear the call of freedom.

The enemy would try to tell you to stay in the cage and remain grounded. But God, the Maker of heaven and earth, created you with divine purpose. The Creator of the universe knit you together in your mother's womb and fashioned you in unique detail and creative design to impact the world with His glory.

There is an anointing over your life. By design, you cannot carry this anointing without God's strength. The anointing oil is heavy, and its refinement comes through significant crushing. Don't fear the crushing; don't allow it to shake your faith. Your trials serve a purpose that will become clear in your calling.

People around you may not understand what God is doing in your life. Learn to accept that. You don't need anyone's permission to shine.

In the book of Genesis, a boy named Joseph is given a God-sized dream and a calling. His dream reveals that he will one day be a ruler and his brothers will bow down to him.

Hearing Joseph's audacious dream, his brothers seek to destroy him in a fit of rabid jealousy. Spared from murder, Joseph is sold into slavery. Even in slavery, Joseph's captivity could not keep him from fulfilling the purpose God had called him to carry out.

Joseph's brothers could not handle his God-sized dream, and their jealousy nearly killed him. Caged by the consequences of their actions, God used Joseph to call them to freedom. *"But Joseph said to them, 'Do not fear, for am I in the place of God? As for you, you meant evil against me, but God meant it for good, to bring it about that many people should be kept alive, as they are today. So do not fear; I will provide for you and your little ones.' Thus he comforted them and spoke kindly to them"* (Genesis 50:19–21 ESV).

Be careful with whom you share your dreams; not everyone will celebrate them. Just as Joseph's brothers tried to imprison him, many will want to restrict your calling or freedom.

Don't forfeit your purpose to please people. Your gifts and calling will make some people squirm. Let them. You don't owe anyone an explanation, nor do you need their approval. Be obedient to the Father's voice; He will handle the jealous spirit that rises against you, which tries to cage you in its limitations.

Seek the Lord, and He will direct your steps. Walk in faith and watch Him part the waters and move the mountains. There is a new sound from heaven, beckoning you to come higher with Him and soar into new elevations. Embrace your calling—your freedom awaits in Christ!

Sister, spread your wings, hit those storms head-on, and allow the momentum of the winds to take you higher!

Key:

When you walk in God's fullness, the oil of His Holy Spirit will flow out of you to advance His kingdom here on earth as it is in heaven. You are a woman of impact and influence. Lift your vision higher.

Action Steps:

1. Invite the Holy Spirit to shatter any man-fearing, man-pleasing spirit in your heart.
2. Ask the Holy Spirit to release a new sound over your life, calling you higher.
3. Pray into those dreams and desires the Lord has placed in your heart.
4. Be intentional. What thought patterns, lies, or old injuries keep you caged up and not walking in your potential?
5. When you read, "Shatter the cage and lift your vision higher," what does that mean to you? Write it out, pray into it, and follow the Holy Spirit's instructions.

2

The Chase

Therefore, behold, I will allure her, and bring her
into the wilderness, and speak tenderly to her.
And there I will give her her vineyards and make the
Valley of Achor a door of hope. And there she shall
answer as in the days of her youth, as at the time
when she came out of the land of Egypt.
(Hosea 2:14–15 ESV)

THE BIBLICAL BOOK of Hosea tells the story of a young woman named Gomer who has lived a life of great promiscuity and destruction, yet God loves her so much that He places her with a kind and caring spouse. This godly man, Hosea, provides her with goodness, safety, provision, and love.

Fully loved, Gomer struggles to rest in this peace and tender care. She leaves her husband and chases the very things that harm her. The numbness doesn't heal her; it furthers her pain as she strays from God's protection.

Gomer seeks money and men—temporary fixes for the hurt that cuts deeply at her soul and sense of self.

In the book of Hosea, God doesn't give up on Gomer, nor does He allow Hosea to give up on her. God pursues Gomer again and again until she accepts the gift of His faithful, pure, and unblemished love. Eventually, Gomer returns to her husband and learns to live in the godly love of her heavenly Father. There, she can finally rest in His peaceful protection and thrive under His grace and mercy.

If I am honest, I have often been just like Gomer. I have seen the truth of God's grace yet have chosen to run from it. And, just as God pursued Gomer, He has never stopped pursuing me.

As a child, I had grown up a Catholic but had never felt a real connection with God. That changed one summer when my neighbor invited me to vacation Bible school. Each day at camp, the youth pastors would share stories about Jesus and how much He loved us. I did not quite understand the love that they were sharing, but it seemed intriguing. One day at the end of our fun activities, the teachers asked us if we wanted to receive Jesus in our hearts and say a prayer. Raising my hand, I prayed and asked Jesus to come into my life. Warmth covered my heart, and absolute peace saturated me. The youth pastor who led me in prayer gave me a Bible titled *Good News for Modern Man*. Once home, I began to read the Bible every chance I could.

Feeling the peace of God contrasted dramatically with the chaos that I knew at home. I recognized God's love was unlike any I had ever known and wanted to learn more.

I voraciously studied my Bible, and as I learned more about Jesus, I became bolder in sharing about Him. This boldness even extended to confronting the monsignor in my Catholic catechism class. My teachers taught me that one must confess to the priest for forgiveness, which contradicted what I read in the Scriptures. I told the monsignor that I did not have to confess to a priest because I could go directly to Jesus! Even then, I had grasped the personal relationship aspect of community with God. I didn't have to go through anyone to get to Him. He was always there for me.

Filled with more questions than answers, I devoured the stories in my Bible. Life did not change at home, but unknowingly to me at the time, the Lord was laying a foundation.

With my growing faith came unusual occurrences that I did not yet understand. I began to have vivid dreams that often came to pass. I would tell my friends about the dreams, and they began to witness them playing out in reality. The frequency of accurate dreams coming to pass became so common that my friends started calling me a witch.

Being called a witch made me feel like a freak, so I began to keep a journal of my dreams instead of sharing them with my friends. I did not realize what was happening, but the Lord was honing a prophetic gift in my life.

Like Gomer, I had seen God's good and loving nature, yet I wasn't ready to rest in His care. My heart drifted as I reached out for other things to numb the pain that my family was putting me through.

In fifth grade, while playing with some friends, someone offered me a beer and a joint, and I took them. A short time later, while doing chores, I discovered a large glass jar filled with green and white capsules. I grabbed a handful and placed them in my pocket. Later, I learned that those pills were drugs called "Christmas trees" and were a type of speed. Little did I know my addiction had begun.

The discovery of the speed soon led me to uncover an even bigger stash. This time, while playing hide and seek,

I found a gold mine of marijuana. Our house didn't offer love, but it seemed to overflow with drugs. I wasn't sure how the drugs were winding up in our house, but this did not stop me from helping myself. It would be years before I learned that my oldest brother was dealing drugs and hiding his stash in the house.

I generously allocated a portion of drugs to myself before disappearing to hang out with some of the notorious trouble-making children in our neighborhood. The buzz dulled the chronic emotional pain I felt, and I was hooked. My casual use of drugs quickly turned into a dependency. Drugs and alcohol had a unique numbing effect that I desired, and I began to crave them more and more. This introduction to drugs and alcohol would be my survival tool for years, and it would become my demise.

I had experienced God yet was lured away by temporary fixes that I falsely thought would fill me. I ran from God, yet He was constantly chasing me. I gave up on God, yet He relentlessly pursued me. Like Gomer, I would experience some hard lessons before fully submitting my life to God. Thankfully, God never gave up on me.

Matthew 18:12–14 (ESV) tells us, *"What do you think? If a man has a hundred sheep, and one of them has gone astray, does he not leave the ninety-nine on the mountains and go in search of the one that went astray? And if he finds it, truly, I say to you, he rejoices over it more than the ninety-nine that never went astray. So it is not the will of my Father who is in heaven that one of these little ones should perish."*

Despite my rejection of God, I am thankful that He never stopped chasing me. Even when I turned my back on Him, God was there.

Key:

You are valuable to God, and He is passionately pursuing you. He loves you beyond measure and desires a relationship with you.

Action Steps:

1. If you are reading this book, recognize that God is already pursuing you!
2. Identify other moments in your life when you have seen glimpses of God.
3. Evaluate the interferences keeping you away from a relationship with the Lord.

4. Ask the Holy Spirit to help you let go of any harmful tendencies.

5. Rest in a relationship with your heavenly Father!

3

Shame Is Not Your Name

In you, O Lord, do I take refuge;
never let me be put to shame.
(Psalm 71:1 ESV)

MY MOM LOVED tea and cigarettes. She smoked two packs of Virginia Slims Menthol a day, the nicotine high acting as a temporary respite from our stressful home life. My mom's hands shook with constant tremors, and cigarettes seemed to be the only vice that settled them to steadiness. My father ridiculed my mom for stuttering and verbally degraded her for nearly everything she did. Most days, she wore her hair in curlers, hidden by a scarf—too emotionally drained to fix it into an attractive style. If my mom ran out of cigarettes, she would verbally lash out in agitation before sending me to the neighbors to mooch money. Money obtained, I would walk to the store and buy her a new supply.

I was deeply humiliated and embarrassed each time I was assigned to plead with the neighbors for funds or purchase my mom's cigs, but I knew it would make her happy. After Mom safely held a new cigarette between her lips, she'd apologize for verbally snapping at me. This was the closest she ever came to expressing any form of love or kindness toward me—her grateful expression of thanks for the new cigarettes.

Often, my mother would scream and rant, telling us children that we had ruined her life. She would yell that the condom broke, that my father raped her, and that she never wanted children. Those words jolted my battered heart every time. They validated the negative thoughts already saturating my mind, telling me I was unwanted. The pain of rejection was overwhelming and polluted my heart. Although she was under tremendous stress with five children and was carrying enormous emotional baggage from her upbringing, I could not comprehend the emotional neglect.

My mom and dad fought incessantly, and I hated it. I tried everything to keep the peace to no avail. As a young girl, I foolishly thought that if I cleaned the whole house and made my parents breakfast in bed, they would be pleased with me. My father responded that the eggs were runny, and my mother's response was I did a half-ass job cleaning. Those words devastated me. I could never figure out why my parents could not show me love or affection. The lack of affirmation and acceptance in my home destroyed my self-worth and kept me locked in a state of insecurity and fear.

My father maintained a gracious front outside our family, but at home, he raged. He once got so angry that he plunged a pitchfork through the liner of our family pool and destroyed it. This level of anger wasn't unusual. It was our normal.

I wet the bed into my teen years due to the constant emotional upheaval; my parent's response was anger and humiliation. I had to sleep on a small cot as punishment. My identity was slowly and methodically deteriorating. When I looked in a mirror, I despised my image and questioned my existence. Unable to process the gross rejection and betrayal, I learned to internalize and blame myself.

A war raged inside me, and I struggled daily with shame, insecurity, and fear. Boundaries did not exist in our home. Our front door did not have a working lock, and the bathroom door was broken and propped up against the wall. There were no curtains in my bedroom, nor did I have a bedroom door. There was nowhere safe.

I was terrified to be left alone with my father—he violated me in the most abhorrent ways. I could not escape or find safety. Whenever my mother left the house, I wept and tried to hide, but my dad always found me. Darkness surrounded my heart when my father hurt me. Nobody knew my secrets, and nobody understood my shame.

Whenever my father violated me, he told me it was my fault. He blamed me for almost any reason, including: I asked him to the father-daughter dance, bathed naked, wanted toys for my birthday, or had been naughty. The shamefulness of his actions was placed on me. For years, fragmented memories haunted my soul, keeping me disconnected from the truth.

The truth was that the shame did not belong to me. The shame that I felt bumming money for my mom's cigarettes—that shame was hers for placing the fulfillment of her addictive needs on a child's shoulders. The shame that I felt for my dad's anger and sexual abuse—that shame belonged to him, the perpetrator of such vile actions.

I carried the shame that belonged to others. Not only did I carry it, but I also began to clothe myself in it. I allowed lies to leach into my heart that I was damaged, unwanted, disgusting, unworthy, and of no value to anyone. I lived these lies in poor decisions that I made in my adulthood. If I couldn't find value in myself, why should anyone treat me as valuable?

Maybe you are struggling with the weight of shame. I want to assure you that Jesus came to set you free! When He died on the cross, He took all your sins and shame upon His sacrifice. It wasn't until many years later that I discovered my true value as a cherished daughter of the King of Kings, and this knowledge transformed my life.

Ephesians 1:4–6 (ESV) tells us, *"Even as he chose us in him before the foundation of the world, that we should be holy and blameless before him. In love he predestined us for adoption to himself as sons through Jesus Christ, according to the purpose of his will, to the praise of his glorious grace, with which he has blessed us in the Beloved."*

Before the beginning of time, God chose you and adopted you as His beloved child. He knows your sin and shame, and yet He covers you in His name!

Key:

You are a child of the King! Shame is not your name or your responsibility to carry.

Action Steps:

1. Identify areas of your life in which you feel bound by shame.
2. Allow yourself to recognize and release the shame.
3. Examine how your life has been shaped by carried shame.
4. Ask the Holy Spirit to reshape you in His image.
5. Walk in victory, knowing that you are a child of the King!

4

Turn toward Freedom

Jesus answered them, "Truly, truly, I say to you,
everyone who practices sin is a slave to sin. The slave does
not remain in the house forever; the son remains forever.
So if the Son sets you free, you will be free indeed.
I know that you are the offspring of Abraham; yet you
seek to kill me because my words find no place in you.
I speak of what I have seen with my Father, and you do
what you have heard from your father."
(John 8:34–38 ESV)

ONCE WHILE ON a missions trip overseas, I heard a story about monkeys trapped and eliminated by poachers. Deep in the jungles of Africa, poachers would set out cages containing food appealing to monkeys. The curious monkeys would cautiously approach the cages, gingerly reaching inside and attempting to grab the food. Once a monkey grasped the food tightly in its clutches, the poachers would rush from their hiding spots and club it to death.

Death was not imminent. The monkey was faster than the poachers and could quickly scurry away on approach. So, what led to the monkey's death? The monkey was held captive by refusing to release the food it was grasping. Clinging to temptation would ultimately result in the monkey's brutal and unnecessary death.

So many times, I have clung to bondage instead of running in freedom. I have stayed in a spot that would ensnare and harm me instead of taking actions that would have led to my release. I accepted lies about who I was instead of the new life offered to me in Christ. Hearing that story, I quickly identified with the monkey.

In my childhood, my parents modeled the example of being a trapped monkey to me. They were both living lives headed toward death and destruction, yet they seemed determined to stay in them even at their peril and mine.

My childhood home was a physical and emotional war zone that offered pain and darkness instead of security. My father was not a nice man, and it seemed I could never obtain his love. My grades were never good enough, the way I cleaned the house was never good enough, and any attempt I made to win his affection was never good enough. Therefore, I believed that I would never measure up or attain approval. Feeling invisible, I would go to school every day with knots in my stomach, longing to escape the reality of my life.

My father was a skilled carpenter whose reputation for excellence was well known. He built houses and unique pieces of furniture. He seemed to find joy in carpentry and coaching sports and expended all his energy toward those investments. My dad showed tremendous love, respect, time, and attention to the boys on his teams, or so it seemed to my neglected heart. He was always working or coaching, but he was unapproachable to me. I often struggled with jealousy as he spent hours with strangers, offering them his best and our family his worst. My father was a cold, callous man who could not see, feel, or connect to my emotional needs. This emotional neglect tormented me. I died a thousand times on the inside growing up.

My mother was twenty-seven when I was born, and I do not doubt that she loved me with all her heart. Unfortunately, she was emotionally unavailable to me as a child due to the severe trauma she endured growing up, compounded by my father's abuse. Her neglect meant that I was often unattended and vulnerable for my father to harm and abuse me.

Given my chaotic home life, I relished experiences that offered normalcy and a chance to be just like any other girl. Every year at the end of our football and cheerleading season, my family attended a banquet to celebrate our accomplishments. We would receive trophies and accolades and have a fun dinner with our teammates and friends. My heart was buzzing with excitement as I anticipated my final banquet. My years cheering for youth football were about to end as I graduated into junior high school. This banquet was a milestone for me, and I was excited to celebrate.

My father's alcoholic rampage changed those plans. Instead of sitting at the table, eating and mingling with family and friends, he isolated himself and drank alcohol at the bar throughout dinner. He was the head football coach, and it was his job to summarize the year, highlight the athletes, and give out awards. As he began to speak, I realized he was not making any sense. He babbled and bumbled through a speech, rambling about unrelated topics, his intoxication evident. I knew something was desperately wrong, and it was apparent to everyone in the room. There was no hiding this—no pretending behind the mask of a charming persona.

As he spoke incoherently, an awkward hush fell over the banquet hall. Another coach from the league escorted my father off the stage, but not without incident. My dad's drunkenness did not stop him from driving us home—we all sat in the car, our bodies rigidly clenched as if braced for impending disaster. Once home and after the front door of our house was closed behind us, all hell broke loose. My dad's mask dropped, and the monster roared forth. He unleashed a violent verbal assault on my mother and older brother before grabbing a rifle and heading out of the house. He set out to punish the man who had removed him from the stage. We all shook with terror and uncertainty, not knowing the outcome of the evening but expecting the worst. What should have been a lovely night with a bit of normalcy turned into a rage-filled evening as we were held hostage by fear.

The following morning, my mother demonstrated the most incredible courage I had ever seen from her. She walked over to the couch where my father had eventually passed out the night before and confronted him: "Are you awake, you bastard?" He mocked her and rolled over. She clenched her teeth, pointed to the door, and demanded

that he leave the house. I was shocked by her fierce forti-
tude; he seemed equally caught off guard by my mother
standing up to him. She refused to back down, and he
left. After that, I rarely saw my dad again.

That was a pivotal moment in my childhood. Before
this, my mother had been much like the monkey clinging
to food and meeting death. She had ignored the dangers
presented by my father to grasp false security. That day,
things were different. She chose freedom.

True freedom for me wouldn't come for years, but that
gave me a glimpse of a different future. I saw that it takes
releasing harm to grasp something better. It takes a bold
step in a different direction to reach a path of freedom.

Key:

Are there habits or relationships you are clinging to
for comfort that are holding you in a pattern of destruction? Are you scared of the changes that bold bravery
may bring?

Action Steps:

1. Identify areas of harm and destruction in your life that seem to be weighing you down.
2. Can you see places of pain where you are clinging to harmful people or situations instead of releasing them and heading in a new direction?
3. Prayerfully make a plan to step into freedom.
4. Make a plan to build firm boundaries from anything keeping you captive.
5. Seek the Holy Spirit and His guidance and protection during the process.

5

El Roi

Then she called the name of the Lord who spoke
to her, You-Are-the-God-Who-Sees; for she said,
"Have I also here seen Him who sees me?"
(Genesis 16:13 NKJV)

IN GENESIS 16, there is a story about a young servant girl named Hagar who has been used and mistreated. She lives in bondage as the Egyptian maidservant of Sarai, Abram's wife. When Sarai cannot conceive a child on her own, she makes a desperate demand. She instructs her husband to have sex with Hagar to impregnate her so that Abram can have offspring. He takes Hagar, and she is given no opportunity to deny this exploitation. She becomes pregnant, fulfilling Sarai's plan, yet this does not assuage her. Sarai becomes bitter and jealous toward Hagar, treating her with malice and hatred. Sarai's vitriol toward Hagar becomes unbearable, and she flees to escape. Rather than continue under Sarai's abuse, Hagar risks death by escaping into the untamed wilderness.

In the barren wilderness, God speaks to Hagar and prophesizes purpose and promise over her life and the life of her unborn child. She replies in awe, giving God the name El Roi, which means the God Who Sees Me. She sought escape, and God answered her with comforting acknowledgment. Hagar did not deserve the terrible treatment she received, yet El Roi, the One Who Sees, fully saw her and her need, revealing Himself to her in her darkest moments. He spoke life into Hagar and gave her beauty from her ashes of despair.

There have been times in my life when, like Hagar, I have felt unseen. I have been hurt and mistreated when I felt desperate to be noticed and heard.

In high school, I was doing drugs and partying hard, trying to fill the void of feeling invisible. As my senior year approached, I knew that changes needed to be made if I wanted to graduate. No longer could I party every day and expect to get good grades; therefore, I decided to stop and to prioritize school.

My older brother discovered Jesus during this time and began inviting me to attend church with him. This church was much different from any solemn Catholic service I attended growing up. It was alive and filled with the rhythms of loud praise and worship while people danced, waved flags, prayed in tongues, prophesied, and demonstrated outward signs of love toward God. I so badly wanted to be loved by God, but I was also afraid to trust His love. I wanted to believe He hadn't forgotten me, so I kept returning to church with my brother. I felt that the Lord saw me there, and my heart began to change. It felt good to be surrounded by God's love, and I longed to remain in it.

I celebrated my high school graduation by returning to my pattern of partying. I still attended church services, yet I felt as if I were in a tug of war between resting in God's love and living a life of pleasurable pursuit. I didn't yet recognize that the peace of being held in the heavenly Father's care was all I truly desired. I mistakenly thought that God's acceptance hinged on my good behavior.

One night after a church service, I stopped by a pizza parlor in my town and laid eyes on the most gorgeous guy I had ever seen! He had long wavy brown hair, moccasin boots, and beautiful brown eyes. We instantly connected as if drawn together by an intense electrical current. This was the first time in my life that I felt seen by anyone, and it was intoxicating. This handsome guy stared into my eyes, and everything in me became alive. I somehow found courage I did not know existed. I invited him to a friend's house after his shift ended, and he accepted. My heart danced and everything else faded. I couldn't believe that he wanted to spend time with me. He showed up that night with pizza, and I provided the beer.

We fell in love and quickly became inseparable. I did not know what love was, but this must be it. My boyfriend's attention became my new addiction.

One night, my new boyfriend and I sat on my front step, talking as I waited to introduce him to my mother for the first time. My mom's car came into sight as it pulled into the driveway. Reading the glare on her face, I could tell she was not in a good mood. She exited the car and headed to the house without looking my way. With great excitement, I called, "Mom, I want you to meet my boyfriend."

This moment was significant for me. I had never dated or gone to my high school dances or prom, but now I had a boyfriend. My mom stared at us before coldly stating, "What are you doing with my daughter? She is a pig."

I sat in stunned silence, pain bleeding out as my mom thrust her massive verbal knife into my heart again. I wanted my mom to see me, share my joy, and accept me, yet she harshly addressed me as I imagined Sarai would have spoken to Hagar.

If my mom could reject me so callously, then surely trying to ever please God was an impossibility. If my parents couldn't love or see me, it was a waste of my time even to consider God would. I decided to reject God before He rejected me. I stopped attending church and returned to my partying lifestyle. How could I have believed that my life would change? Endless pain seemed to be my portion, so I stopped hoping for anything else.

I longed to be seen by God but accepted my boyfriend as a substitute filler for all the hurting wounds leaking from my damaged heart. Within a few months of dating, I began feeling persistent nausea that plagued me daily. I first blamed my queasy stomach on the cheap beer I had been drinking, yet the ill feeling never seemed to disappear. Eventually, I took a pregnancy test, and the result was positive, to my surprise.

I was barely out of high school, yet I was about to have a baby. My five-month pregnancy bump was already appearing when my boyfriend and I chose to get married. I hoped marriage and a baby would somehow manufacture a happy home for myself. Little did I realize when we said, "For better, for worse," how much worse life could become.

Like Hagar, I had experienced pain and mistreatment in my life while I longed to be seen. However, instead of running to the wilderness and finding El Roi, I had hidden from God in the arms of a man who would hurt and abandon me. As a teenage mom, I thought God could not see past mistakes. I thought that He would see me only if I were good enough, but the truth is that God already saw me. He saw my hurt, pain, rejection, and sadness, and He still loved me. He loved me right where I was. He saw me and called me to come with Him, but I wasn't ready to receive His love. I wasn't ready to recognize that the God Who Sees saw me and had a prophecy of promise waiting to speak over my life.

Key:

Do you believe that God can use all the ugliness in your life for His glory? If not, why not? If you do, then release everything to Him, trusting that He is painting a beautiful story from the pieces of your past.

Action Steps:

1. Read Genesis 16 and meditate on the name El Roi, the One Who Sees. Ask God to bring remembrance of all the times He saw you in your darkest moments when you wanted to give up and flee.

2. Lift a shout of praise with great gratitude that God has been faithful throughout your life. Even in the bleakest moments, He is El Roi, the God Who Sees, and He won't leave you abandoned.

3. Look in a mirror and declare these words over yourself: "I am forgiven, accepted, celebrated, affirmed, and loved by God."

4. Be intentional and forgive those who have spoken painful words over your life.

5. Ask God to heal every soul wound and to heal others through your testimony.

6

A Call to Surrender

Agree with God, and be at peace; thereby good
will come to you. Receive instruction from his mouth,
and lay up his words in your heart. If you return
to the Almighty you will be built up; if you remove
injustice far from your tents.
(Job 22:21–23 ESV)

FOR YEARS, I was bound by destructive habits, crying to God for deliverance, but the clutches of darkness mocked my cries. Enshrined in addiction, I begged, pleaded, and called on the Lord to set me free. I believed in God's sovereignty and often scribbled illegible notes to Him in my journal, hoping He would hear me. Addictions encapsulated my soul and rendered me ineffective.

I experienced dreams and visions that manifested in reality, and I knew God was speaking to me, but I raged at Him to leave me alone. I knew I had a prophetic gift through His visions, but these dreams disconcerted me as I didn't yet see God's purpose in them. I was playing a game of tug-of-war with myself. I would call for God to save me while pushing His words and wisdom away. Pulling my addictions closer, I would blame God for the destruction that I was causing myself. I did not fully understand that He had given me gifts that were not contingent on my behavior but were gifted through His faithfulness.

One day with rock-'n'-roll blasting through the house and empty beer bottles scattered in every room, I chugged the beer in my hand and then began to sweep the dining room floor. My mind wandered through scattered thoughts as I swept under the cabinet with my old tattered broom. As I pulled the broom toward me to gather the dust bunnies and cobwebs that had been accumulating under the cabinet, I was surprised to see a dusty cassette tape emerge. The tape, titled *Radically Saved*, was by a Christian singer named Carman.

I wondered who Carman was and how this tape ended up in my house. We had an extensive music collection, but this particular tape was not part of it. Perplexed, I inserted it into our stereo system, and his words pierced the atmosphere, commanding my attention. The first song that belted out of the worn cassette was an upbeat, enthusiastic tune called "I've Been Delivered." It told the stories of people who were set free from the bonds of sickness, disease, and death. Jesus delivered them from the impossible, and this pulled at my heart.

Immediately I felt something inside demanding that I shut it off. A different voice, full of peace and care deep in my soul, was drawn to the music. Little did I know the words were shifting the atmosphere in my home as God interrupted my chaos with His divine destiny. This nudge that I felt had me rewinding the song, playing it over and over again.

Two months later, my sister-in-law invited me to a Christian ladies' breakfast at a local hotel. I agreed to join her, but I stayed up late the night before the meeting, drinking whiskey and beer and snorting cocaine. When she picked me up the following day, I did not realize that the trajectory of my life was about to change. Sitting in that room, I tried to listen, but I was so strung out and exhausted that it was difficult to focus. After the woman at the microphone completed her message, my sister-in-law took me up for prayer. These women began praying in other tongues and pleading to God on my behalf. They saw through my façade and stood in the gap, interceding for my deliverance. I returned to the breakfast meetings several times but did not recognize the spiritual setup.

I knew God. He was chasing me relentlessly. I was calling out for rescue, and He was sending help. He offered deliverance, yet I was still not ready to submit to Him. I clung to my addiction and relied on myself without realizing that if I surrendered to God, He could do so much more than I could do on my own failing strength.

I was crying to be rescued while turning my back on the rescue He sent. Thankfully, we serve a God who never gives up on us.

Romans 8:13–17 (ESV) says, *"For if you live according to the flesh you will die, but if by the Spirit you put to death the deeds of the body, you will live. For all who are led by the Spirit of God are sons of God. For you did not receive the spirit of slavery to fall back into fear, but you have received the Spirit of adoption as sons, by whom we cry, 'Abba! Father!' The Spirit himself bears witness with our spirit that we are children of God, and if children, then heirs—heirs of God and fellow heirs with Christ, provided we suffer with him in order that we may also be glorified with him."*

I had been adopted by Christ and called His own, yet instead of walking in His Spirit, I was walking in the slavery of my addictions. The Lord was giving me a path to life, yet I was choosing a slow spiritual and physical death. A patient Father, God was offering me a way rich in His goodness, but I had the freedom to choose or reject it.

Key:

God has a better way for you—it is your choice to surrender.

Action Steps:

1. Identify moments in your life when you have seen God calling you.
2. Take the time to write down moments when you have heard God's voice.
3. Look at this list and examine the things that have stopped you from pursuing a life in the Spirit. Are these things helping or harming you?
4. Write a second list that names people who have intervened, encouraging you to walk closer to the Lord.

5. Be brave and reach out to one of the people you have listed. Meet for coffee or a quick phone call and ask him or her to walk beside you in your journey to grow in the Lord.

7

Goaded by Grace

And I said, "Who are you, Lord?" And the Lord said,
"I am Jesus whom you are persecuting. But rise and
stand upon your feet, for I have appeared to you for this
purpose, to appoint you as a servant and witness to the
things in which you have seen me and to those in which I
will appear to you, delivering you from your people and
from the Gentiles—to whom I am sending you to open
their eyes, so that they may turn from darkness
to light and from the power of Satan to God,
that they may receive forgiveness of sins and a place
among those who are sanctified by faith in me."
(Acts 26:15–18 ESV)

ONE OF THE most dynamic apostles in the biblical
New Testament church was a man named Paul, who
initially fiercely fought to destroy Christians. A Pharisee
who before his conversion was called Saul, Paul was a
Jewish leader who did not believe in the resurrection of

Christ. Beyond simple disbelief was intense hatred. He hunted down Christians to imprison, torture, and have them killed. He was intent on destroying this newfound Christianity that was spreading like wildfire.

On a trip to the city of Damascus to destroy more Christians, Paul was stopped by a bright light and the voice of Jesus: *"And when we had fallen to the ground, I heard a voice saying to me in the Hebrew language, 'Saul, Saul, why are you persecuting me? It is hard for you to kick against the goads'"* (Acts 26:14 ESV).

If you have heard this story before, you may have missed that ending statement, "It is hard for you to kick against the goads." What does this mean? In Paul's time, oxen were driven or guided by slender wooden rods, which often ended in a point. They were made to nudge oxen in the direction they were to go. Stubborn oxen would kick against the goads, injuring themselves on the sharpened points in the process.

The Bible passage emphasizing Paul kicking against the goads tells us that this miraculous encounter on the road to Damascus wasn't the first time that Paul had felt the nudge of Christ. We can surmise from the text that Paul had been kicking at the prodding of the Spirit for a while, ignoring God's voice and chasing destruction.

I can relate. In my own life, I had long heard the voice of Jesus, only to ignore it while embracing temporary fixes to hide, not heal, the holes in my life.

With my ninth wedding anniversary fast approaching, I was busy planning our family vacation to Lake Ontario, Canada. My in-laws owned a sweet rustic cabin directly on the water, and we were going to drive and spend a week there.

It wasn't our first visit to the cabin. The previous year we had vacationed there, the magnificent beauty of our surroundings marred by our excessive drinking that stretched from morning to night. Our out-of-control alcoholism scared me for the safety of our children. On the last day of that visit, as I packed the van to return to New Jersey, I gazed at the vast lake and beautiful scenery and knew in my heart that we would not make it back to that cabin again.

As I continued planning our next vacation, I again felt that same strong sense of not returning, but I pushed that feeling aside. The nudges in my heart were hushed as I tried to make my preparations.

Two weeks before our scheduled vacation, my husband made plans for his mother to watch the children the night before our anniversary. I assumed my husband had special plans to celebrate. Instead, as we sat on our back steps, he told me he did not love me and gave me his wedding ring.

I drank to mask the denial and woke up the following day, assuming it was all a nightmare. It was a nightmare—one that was true. My husband was leaving me. My soul plummeted into despair and desperation. I was swallowed up by confusion, chaos, and pain. *What did he mean he did not love me? Leaving? How could this happen?* My husband—my best friend, the one person who knew everything about me—was abandoning me. Once again, I felt I was not good enough, which was devastating.

My husband packed a small toiletry bag and went to his mother's house. His mother knew about this plan. She embraced the idea and let him move home.

He started attending parties and quickly moved in with a nineteen-year-old girl, her son, and her family a few minutes away from our home. I felt as if he had replaced our family without a second thought. *Help! Somebody tell me how to breathe!* I could not wrap my mind around the rejection and abandonment.

My father and I had not spoken in years, and my mother lived in Arizona with her new husband. My sister lived in California, and my brothers were scattered around New Jersey. I had nowhere to go and felt as if I had no one to turn to. I was shattered into a million pieces and paralyzed with fear again.

I sought help from my family doctor, who recommended counseling. Interestingly, the only counseling practice my insurance covered was a drug and alcohol addiction center near my home. The intake forms were extensive, and I was candid in answering the questions about my drug and alcohol use for the first time in my life. Out of a comprehensive questionnaire, I could respond "no" to only one question: whether I ever had a DWI (driving while intoxicated) arrest. I proudly held on to that one answer, proving that I was not an alcoholic or drug addict. I failed to immediately recognize that I had not driven more than a couple of blocks during our marriage.

The counselor looked me straight in the eyes and said, "You don't have a DWI *yet*, but if you keep drinking the way you are drinking, you will." He also strongly suggested I attend Alcoholics Anonymous (AA) meetings, which I thought was ridiculous. I was seeing a counselor only in an attempt to get my husband back. Nothing else mattered beyond that. Why couldn't the counselor see that and wave his magic wand to accomplish what I wanted?

After I was done with every lame excuse, he told me to try six AA meetings, and if I did not feel I had an addiction issue after attending six sessions, I did not have to return.

I attended my first meeting that Sunday night, and as I walked in, sat down, and listened, I knew I was in the right place and had a tiny spark of hope.

That night, I threw away my last six-pack of beer, nice and neat, into the trash can. I stood the beers up straight just in case I changed my mind. Having a plan B in recovery is never a good idea in case you change your mind—which I did. A few nights later, I took those beers out of the trash can and drank them. It was not enough alcohol to get me drunk, but it was enough to make me sick.

Early the next morning, at 3:00 A.M., I was awakened by an epiphany. My life was a mess, and it was nobody else's fault but mine. I saw an image of my dog chasing her tail. The dog would exhaust herself, trying to catch something that could never be caught. In the same fashion, I had exhausted myself, blaming everyone else in my life for my pain and my choices. The struggles were real; the pain was raw, and I no longer had a crutch to hide behind. My excuses were gone. All I had now was a mirror and a choice to be made.

This was my Damascus road experience; this was the wake-up call I needed to change my life drastically. Like the apostle Paul, I had been kicking at the proverbial goads for years, and my only accomplishments were pain and destruction to myself and to everyone around me. My childhood family had caused a lot of pain and hurt, but I was an adult now. The decisions that I had been making were causing harm to my children and to myself. I had to change. I had to choose. There were no more excuses, only the exhausted relief of collapsing into the comforting arms of Jesus.

Key:

Your calling starts when your self-capacity ends— when you realize that trying it your way will fail, and you fall into the grace and mercy of the Holy Spirit.

Action Steps:

1. Pray. Ask the Lord to show you destructive areas you need to turn away from, examine these areas, and accept responsibility for your actions.
2. Breathe. Give yourself grace, and know that God gives you more grace than you can fathom.
3. Seek wise counsel and prayer to learn how to remove hurtful or harmful addictive behaviors or patterns from your life.
4. Recognize that God is not trying to harm you but to protect you from yourself.
5. Know that you are cherished and deeply loved by God.

8

Cast the First Stone

But God shows his love for us in that while
we were still sinners, Christ died for us.
(Romans 5:8 ESV)

LOVE SPOKE. Humiliated. Exposed. Condemned. A woman caught in the act of adultery is paraded through the streets by an angry mob. Clutching desperately at hurriedly gathered scraps of clothing or perhaps covered only in her shame, she is scorned as the crowd calls for her to be stoned. The Pharisees and scribes revel in ruling as judge and jury for her sin. Jeering and taunting, they cast her at the feet of Jesus, their hands gripped tightly around the stones they intended to hurl. Sin demands sacrifice, and condemnation is what they call for. Their prideful, self-righteous hearts disdainfully call for the woman to pay the cost of her sin in death, while Jesus replies with loving, life-bringing conviction. The scribes and Pharisees seek to validate their judgment, but Jesus calls them to examine their own hearts.

Then the scribes and Pharisees brought to Him a woman caught in adultery. And when they had set her in the midst, they said to Him, "Teacher, this woman was caught in adultery, in the very act. Now Moses, in the law, commanded us that such should be stoned. But what do You say?" This they said, testing Him, that they might have something of which to accuse Him.

But Jesus stooped down and wrote on the ground with His finger, as though He did not hear.

So when they continued asking Him, He raised Himself up and said to them, "He who is without sin among you, let him throw a stone at her first."

(John 8:3–7 NKJV).

Jesus demolished their intentions with one statement: "He who is without sin among you, let him throw a stone at her first." Jesus was not entrapped with enticing words of contention but responded gently by pointing out the glaring truth that not one of them was without sin. Jesus did not shame, humiliate, or parade their sin to be exposed—He spoke softly, convicting them to examine their hearts. One by one, the mob disbanded as the silent rebuke hung in the air. Love spoke, dismantling their hate—and love continues to speak more than 2,000 years later.

There was a time in my life when my pockets were heavy with stones that I cast at everyone around me. I was miserable and blamed others for my mess. It was easy to criticize others when I ignored my own sin inventory. I cast blame on everyone around me without reflecting on the responsibility that I bore. Throwing rocks was far more manageable than taking ownership of my reckless choices.

One day I sat on my couch, paralyzed by emotional pain and confusion, crying out to God for help. I was newly sober and furious at my husband for abandoning my two sons and me. I was mad at his family for turning their backs on me, and I wanted someone to pay for my pain. I was angry at everyone and wallowing in self-pity. God knew what they had done to me, and I was convinced He would call for their stoning. They had hurt me—this deserved a punishing rebuke or painful penalty.

Instead of answering my call for revenge, the Lord sent Cindy, a Christian sister who spoke truth into my life. After I paraded my husband's sins for her to judge, I expected her to pat me on the back and join me in the stoning. Instead, Cindy dared to tell me that I needed to repent for the hate and unforgiveness I carried in my heart. My friend explained that God had forgiven me all my sins and that I needed to throw away the stones I was collecting.

This reaction shook me. I was upset that Cindy didn't pacify me. Did she not understand how badly I was mistreated? Could she see my heart bleeding from the wounds?

She did. Cindy saw my hurt, anger, and anguish, but she also saw a higher reality: God's truth.

She looked at me and asked a powerful, life-changing question: "Do you want to be right, or do you want to be free?"

I chose freedom. I was weighed down by the stones in my grasp, and to be free, I needed to release them. I needed to entrust the situation to the Lord.

Cindy prayed, and as she did, I wept as I asked God for forgiveness. The heavy chains of hate fell from my heart, and I experienced freedom for the first time in many years. The Holy Spirit transformed my living room into Holy Ground, and a divine encounter became a defining moment in my life. The light of Christ shone in the darkest parts of my soul, setting me free.

Then Jesus spoke to them again, saying,
"I am the light of the world. He who follows Me shall not
walk in darkness but have the light of life."

(John 8:12 NKJV)

Key:

You are called to love your enemies. It's easy to love those who love you—you can do that in your own strength. You need the supernatural love of God to help you love those who have hurt you. This does not mean allowing those who hurt you to continue to cause you pain. It simply means releasing the bitter burden you hold against them and entrusting God with their accountability and care. It is judging and maintaining your heart instead of seeking to inflict your condemnation on others.

Action Steps:

1. Schedule uninterrupted time with the Lord and have your journal, pen, and Bible ready.
2. Ask the Holy Spirit to search your heart and show you any offense or unforgiveness you are carrying.

3. Be quick to repent, and ask the Lord to fill you to overflowing with His love.

4. Pray for those who have hurt you. Ask God to bless them.

5. Give the hurt, offense, and hate to God. Choose to lay it down.

6. Invite the Holy Spirit to heal your heart. Our pain often blinds us, keeping us trapped.

9

F.E.A.R.

Assuredly, I say to you, whatever you bind on earth
will be bound in heaven, and whatever you loose
on earth will be loosed in heaven.
(Matthew 18:18 NKJV)

WHILE SITTING IN the stark rooms of an Alcoholics Anonymous (AA) meeting, I first heard the acronym F.E.A.R.—False Evidence Appearing Real. It reverberated in my heart, jolting me to my core. I did not know how to live fear-free. Fear had been my constant companion, and I could not imagine functioning without it. Fear was the filter that I viewed life through daily, my decisions sifted through a lying lens polluted with stinking thinking and irrational thoughts.

For as long as I can remember, I lived bound by fear. As a small child, I feared my father's unpredictable anger. As I grew, I feared who would enter my bedroom at night.

I feared death, darkness, and abandonment. Fear became the compass by which I navigated my life.

As a young mother, I feared harm coming upon my children. I also feared my husband leaving me or dying from an overdose. As a single mother, decisions were made based on the counsel of fear instead of the wisdom of truth. As I cowered in the consultation of the lying lead of fear, I was stripped of boldness.

Fear dominated every facet of my life. I was afraid of going outside in the dark—terrified of coming home and finding an intruder hiding in one of my closets. I slept with a butcher knife under my pillow, regularly dialing 9-1-1 because of the sounds I heard at night. When I walked to my car, I was convinced someone was lying under it or hiding in the backseat. Fear had grasped me as a child, but I gripped it back at some point, refusing to let it go.

I was serving in a Spirit-filled church, reading and singing about the freedom of Christ, but secretly I was living a double life of a Christian woman bound by fear and riddled with anxiety. Nighttime was the most difficult as nightmares plagued my sleep, terrorizing me as I fought to find respite. Attempting to cry for help, I felt choked by invisible hands that kept my screams from escaping. Terrified, I stayed awake at night until I passed out from utter weariness, hoping the lack of sleep would not impact my job performance the following day. If I did manage to collapse into an exhaustion-fueled escape into sleep, I would wake up shaking, sweating, and gasping for breath. Whether waking or sleeping, there was no peace or reprieve from the pursuit of fear.

I felt crazy, wondering if I would ever walk in freedom. Was it even possible to live without fear? Shame held me in a chokehold from daring to ask anyone for help or tell them my secret.

One day, a friend randomly gave me a Bible verse she felt the Lord wanted me to know: *"For God has not given us a spirit of fear, but of power and of love and of a sound mind"* (2 Timothy 1:7 NKJV).

Did she or anyone else know the battle I was facing? How could she have possibly known how badly I needed that truth to be confirmed in my life?

I held onto that verse like a drowning person would cling to a life preserver in the middle of the ocean. Every morning and every night, I read 2 Timothy 1:7, marinating my heart in the truths of God, crying out for Him to heal me. Nothing changed immediately, but gradually that fear began to break, and my life began to radically change. As I reached out for the hand and healing of the Holy Spirit, I released the grip that fear had gained. I was set free of fear and wrapped in the goodness and grace of God's truth.

Today, I live fear-free and no longer find myself bound by the lies and torment that once dominated my life. Fear is a liar, and fear is false evidence appearing real. Freedom is possible with Christ!

Make no mistake that thoughts of fear still come at me, but now I recognize those unhealthy, demonic influences and take those thoughts captive to the obedience of Christ, and I walk in freedom.

Key:

As a believer, you have authority. Take every thought of fear that comes against you and measure it to the Word of God. What does God say about fear? Pick up your sword (the Word of God) and tear those lies down!

Action Steps:

1. Pray and ask the Holy Spirit to reveal the areas in your heart where fears live. Ask Him to uncover the root of the fear.
2. Ask yourself if you are 100 percent certain that your fear is valid.
3. Repent, surrender, and receive healing from all fear.
4. Pay attention to the words you speak. Be careful not to come into agreement with fear.
5. Create a space to spend time with the Holy Spirit and have a notebook and pen ready to hear and write what He shows you.
6. Choose to walk in freedom. It's yours!

10

Ditch the Excuses

Know this, my beloved brothers:
let every person be quick to hear,
slow to speak, slow to anger.
(James 1:19 ESV)

DO YOU TYPICALLY react or respond to circumstances? Do you know the difference? When you react, you hand over your power. When you respond, you remain in control over your actions.

I was a reactor for many years, and my emotions dictated my response, which landed me in many uncomfortable and painful situations. I would lash out and justify my behavior if someone triggered me.

In hindsight, I understand the root cause of my former actions and reactions. Through years of abuse and neglect growing up, I learned to live in survival mode, which meant I was easily triggered, and the mere sense of emotional danger sent me into a tizzy. There was always a sense that I needed to protect myself. Therefore, I was slow to listen, quick to speak, and quick to anger, the exact opposite of scripture.

I illustrated this reactionary behavior shortly after my first husband had abandoned our nine-year marriage, and I learned he had been having an affair. One night, I followed him to a parking lot, where I spotted his girl-friend's car. Devastated and angry by his betrayal, my emotions were out of control.

My husband stood in front of my car to keep me from leaving, assuming I would not drive away. He misjudged me. I put my foot on the gas, and he landed on the hood against my windshield.

Our two young sons were in the car with me, but my out-of-control emotions overrode any common sense or self-discipline. I eventually stopped the vehicle, and by the grace of God, no physical harm was done. No doubt, I emotionally scarred my sons by reacting like a lunatic. The fact that my husband had abandoned our marriage and moved in with someone else and her son fueled me for revenge, and I felt justified in doing what I did, but I was wrong. I deeply regret my reaction that night.

I learned the hard way that if you don't master your emotions, your emotions will master you. Thank God, today, thirty years later, my sons and I laugh about that situation. I am not sure if their father is laughing, but he is alive. My knee-jerk reaction could have caused a tragedy that night.

As a Christian, you are growing in the image of Christ every day, and the way you respond to your pain and trials is essential. The Lord is not as interested in rescuing you from your pain as He is in fashioning your heart after His.

God created your emotions, and He has emotions, but you cannot allow them to dictate your decisions and actions. Your feelings are fickle and change daily. Your compass must always be the Word of God and His counsel, not your feelings.

You have a spirit, a soul, and a body. When you are born again, you receive a new Spirit, but you still carry your soul, which houses your emotions, traumas, disappointments, and pain. Can you see why it's essential that you seek the Holy Spirit's counsel? The Spirit of God is in you, and His ways are much higher than yours. When you learn to respond to situations, you allow your spirit to override your soul. Therefore, your emotions are subject to the Spirit of God, not the other way around.

You may struggle with your emotions when encountering a situation that "feels" unfair or unjust.

In Acts 16, we learn that the Apostle Paul received a heavenly vision directing him to visit Macedonia to preach the Gospel. Once there, a young slave girl, filled with a spirit of divination, brought her masters much money by fortune-telling, and she followed Paul and Silas around the city.

For many days, the girl trailed after the men of God, crying out, "These are servants of the Most High God." Finally, Paul became greatly annoyed, and wanting to end her cries, he cast the spirit of divination out of her. Paul healed her with power from the Holy Spirit, yet those who made money from her were incensed.

The slave girl's divinations made them significant income, yet now that she was free of them, she could no longer function for their profitability. Her masters reacted in great anger. They dragged Paul and Silas to the magistrate, accusing them of disrupting the city. The crowd was irate and out of control, and the magistrate called for the men of God to suffer fierce beatings by rods and imprisonment in the inner prison cell, fastened in stocks.

Two innocent men, obeying the Lord, were beaten and thrown into the inner prison, yet they did not react;

they responded in praise. Their suffering wasn't fair, and the accusations were not true, but they warred from a place of intimacy, not emotion. Despite their circumstances, they worshipped with all their heart.

Paul and Silas responded in faith. God responded to their faith with His faithfulness.

The trials you endure are not meant to destroy you but to build your faith, to fashion you in God's image, and to glorify Him.

Key:

God has given you the capacity for emotion. Yet you should never consult your emotions as the source for your response to your circumstances, and you should never react without giving the situation some space.

Action Steps: Practice these when faced with challenging situations.

1. Stop and take a few deep breaths.
2. Access the situation and ask yourself:

- Can I say with 100 percent certainty that my emotions are the truth?
- If so, what does that mean? Am I willing to trust God?

3. Invite the Holy Spirit's wisdom.
4. Give it time.
5. Thoughtfully respond.
6. Acknowledge that you may not be able to change the situation, but you can handle it with grace and wisdom.

11

Imposter Syndrome

For if you keep silent at this time,
relief and deliverance will rise for the Jews from another
place, but you and your father's house will perish.
And who knows whether you have not come to the
kingdom for such a time as this?
(Esther 4:14 ESV)

THE BOOK OF Esther tells of a Jewish orphan girl who becomes queen of all of Persia. Given favor by the king, she is placed in a role of esteem. Yet, Esther hesitates to act when she receives the word that her people, the Jews, are to be destroyed and annihilated in a plot against them. Although God has placed her in a role that would allow her to speak out in the protection of her people, she's scared. She doesn't recognize that God has placed her in this position for a purpose and reason. He has ordained her as queen "for such a time as this."

When Esther embraces her calling and acts boldly, her people are saved. However, to accomplish this, she must walk in the confidence of a queen instead of the timidity of an orphan child.

Although little girls often play-act the role of queens or princesses, the reality is that many of us claim the qualifications of an orphan spirit over our lives. We view ourselves through the lens of rejection, shame, abandonment, or disappointment instead of defining ourselves as a new creation in Christ. Orphans no longer, we are daughters of the King, adopted under His Holy name. We need to walk in the power of our divine title!

As a single mother struggling to build a new life from the debris of my first marriage, I was so used to living in bondage that I didn't recognize its grip on my life. After my divorce, as I worked to restore my future, I began working as a project secretary at a large construction management firm. I loved my job and was tenacious and determined. I wanted to excel and establish a future for myself and my children. I began attending school at the prestigious Drexel University, taking construction management classes to grow and accomplish more in my job field. While I remained a secretary, my capacity at the company was limited. Without a degree, there seemed no path for me to move up or gain a promotion.

I was willing to work hard to earn accomplishments, so I resolved to do just that. I took additional classes and increased my job responsibilities. While raising my children, I worked doggedly, sacrificing my weekends and holidays to contribute more to my company. Hunger for success drove me, and eventually, my efforts paid off when the company's vice president took notice.

One day, the vice president and project manager took me out to lunch to discuss my future in the company. Our company had a clearly defined path for promotion, beginning at the entry-level position I held as a project secretary. The next tier was to become a project engineer, and following successful service in that position, I could work my way to manager. My degree in construction management remained incomplete, yet I was filled with audacious courage when asked about my future goals.

The vice president asked me, "Kelly, where do you see yourself in this company in five years, ten years, and twenty years?"

Maintaining direct eye contact, I assertively stated, "First, I see myself as a project engineer, then I see myself as a project manager, and eventually, I see myself sitting in your position as vice president of this company."

My brash declaration delighted the company VP. He loved my tenacious boldness and was wise enough to know that I could accomplish my goals without threatening his position's security.

I serve a God of the impossible, and in doing so, God made my promotion to project engineer possible, although I did not have the academic qualifications for the position. I was well compensated, respected, and esteemed in my new role.

I had worked incredibly hard, and God had poured out His great favor on me, allowing me to step into the role that He had readied me for. Yet my response was to reduce and minimize God's gift. When people would ask me my job title, instead of proudly declaring it as I had boldly asserted my aspirations to the VP, I would shy away and minimize it by qualifying it with explanations. When asked, I would state, "I'm a project engineer, but not really a *project engineer*." I would over-explain instead of owning the role God had placed me in. I had great favor, yet I began grappling with imposter syndrome.

I could identify what I was doing, but I didn't realize that this was a form of bondage, holding me back from my full potential. This struggle with imposter syndrome—undervaluing my competence and God-given qualifications—carried over into my ministry. When I received my special ministry license, I would not tell anyone out of fear and anxiety. When I became an ordained minister, I thought, "I can't tell anyone because I am not a real minister."

Do you see how this mindset held me in bondage? When God ordains you for a specific purpose, and you shrink from acknowledging the miraculous arrangement of this calling, do you see how that diminishes the testimony of what God has completed in your life? Imposter syndrome keeps you from stepping into your fullest potential. It holds you back from everything that God has created you to become. To ignite your purpose, you need to clothe yourself in God's calling. You need to claim His freedom over your life and His definition of who He has created you to be!

Can you imagine if Queen Esther had remained bound by imposter syndrome? What if she stayed silent as her people were murdered? But she spoke out for her people's protection by stepping into her God-ordained role as the queen.

What are you shrinking from? Can you identify areas where you shy away from the very things God has provided you? As women, we often do this without thinking about it. A compliment such as "Kelly, I love your shirt" is usually immediately followed by a qualifier instead of grateful acceptance: "Oh, this shirt? It was only one dollar at the thrift store." We diminish the compliment and unconsciously embrace imposter syndrome instead of walking confidently in the character of our Creator.

When God places you in a role that He has prepared you for, it is your responsibility to walk in your calling confidently. He has made you for a time such as this—the King Himself has called you. There's no greater endorsement than that. Walk boldly in the position that Christ has purposed you for!

Ephesians 2:10 (ESV) tells us, *"For we are his workmanship, created in Jesus Christ for good works, which God prepared beforehand, that we should walk in them."* Walk boldly!

Key:

Embrace your calling. The Kings of kings has placed you where you are for a purpose, and He has equipped you.

Action Steps:

1. Write down, "I am a daughter of the King of Kings!"
2. Declare, "The Lord has qualified me for His calling."
3. Identify areas where you diminish what God has done by minimizing His accomplishments in your life.
4. Ask the Holy Spirit to fill you with His power so you may walk in supernatural boldness, fulfilling God's purpose for your life.

12

Imperfect People, Perfect God

I will give you a new heart and put a new spirit
within you; I will take the heart of stone out of your flesh
and give you a heart of flesh. I will put My Spirit
within you and cause you to walk in My statutes,
and you will keep My judgments and do them.
(Ezekiel 36:26–27 NKJV)

PERFECT RELATIONSHIPS ARE for fairy tales.

My relationship with my parents and siblings was complicated. We all had lived in survivor mode for so long that our family dynamic was severely fragmented. Years of pain and abuse had eroded trust, and none of us had a solid foundation for a relationship with one another. Sometimes we would try, but it was a constant cycle of hurt and alienation, and we all retreated to our vices of choice to deal with our broken family structure.

When my husband bailed on our marriage, it was a significant wake-up call for me. Crushing waves of despair paralyzed me, and I had never felt more alone. My mother and three of my siblings lived in other states, and we were not close enough physically or emotionally for me to lean on them, so I learned to rely on God.

God started to restore the wasteland of my soul and reframe my life. Through counseling, prayer, recovery groups, and church, I began to learn and institute boundaries for the first time and to guard my sanity against emotionally unsafe people. My mind started to heal, and cycles of defeat began to break. Hell was no longer my home, addiction was not my friend, and dysfunction was no longer my portion.

I drew a line of demarcation in the spiritual realm and learned how to disrupt the generational sins and cycles so I could walk in freedom and clear a pathway for my children to walk in theirs.

The Holy Spirit performed supernatural heart surgery and gave me the capacity to forgive my parents, which created space for a level of restoration. Forgiveness was a complex and exhausting process and a choice of obedience. God gave me a willing heart.

For many years, I had to mentally prepare myself before spending time with either of my parents, for they were still toxic on some level to me. I was easily triggered and needed to detox emotionally after most visits. I often cried out to God, asking if our relationship could ever be normal or healthy.

My dad had stopped drinking alcohol years prior, and the Lord was softening his heart. He never asked for forgiveness from me, nor did we ever speak about the pain of my childhood. I found tremendous healing and growth, but I always grieved not having a father who adored and affirmed me. I still do.

I saw my father often during the final years of his life and found peace and acceptance with him. He had macular degeneration and could not drive, so I took him to many of his appointments. Although I no longer viewed him as a threat, I maintained firm boundaries and did not leave my children alone with him.

Buying a Father's Day or birthday card was always challenging. I could not lie and buy a card that read, "To the best father in the world, who showed me love and was always there for me." But I could honor him by saying, "Happy Father's Day" and that I loved him.

For Christmas one year, I gave my dad a replica of Thomas Blackshear's painting, *Forgiven*. In the picture, Jesus is holding a worn-out man with large nails and a hammer in his hands, representing all of humanity whose sin nailed him to the cross. For the longest time, my father did not display the picture, and I believe the reason is that he had not forgiven himself and struggled to accept God's forgiveness. One day while visiting, *Forgiven* was sitting on his television cabinet. At that moment, I felt that my dad had embraced the beautiful message of the cross.

A few years before my mother passed away, we talked about all the abuse from my father and others. She was shocked and was crying. Up to that point, she had believed that my childhood was without incident. I told my mom that nobody escapes the smoke when a house is on fire.

When I was younger, I found the courage to tell her about one incident, but she did not believe me, so I never spoke about the abuse again. When I was fifteen, her boyfriend abused me, and he convinced her it was my fault, so she kicked me out of the house. It was easier to detach and numb myself than deal with the reality that my mother would not protect me. My mom lived in denial because she had never received healing from all her childhood trauma. As an adult, I understood that, but as a little girl, I couldn't wrap my mind or heart around it.

My mom carried a tremendous weight of regret and trauma, and I begged her to receive counseling so she could live in freedom, but she would not.

Despite the messy dynamics, the Lord continued to heal our hearts. As we grew older, my mother became my greatest cheerleader and adored me. She bragged about me to all her friends and never missed an opportunity to tell me how proud she was.

In my mother's final moments on this earth, I sobbed by her bedside. I saw so much beauty and strength in her eyes that somehow previously escaped me. She had caressed and kissed my face when I was born, and now I was caressing and kissing her face as she passed on to Glory. I was devastated but very grateful that the Lord had restored our hearts to one another before taking her home.

One of my mother's favorite prayers was the Aaronic blessing; she would pray it over me when we spoke on the phone. If you have never received a father's blessing, I encourage you to read this prayer and allow the words to penetrate your heart as a blessing from your heavenly Father:

Adonai bless you and keep you!
Adonai make His face to shine on you
and be gracious to you!
Adonai turn His face toward you
and grant you shalom!
(Numbers 6:24–26 TLV)

God created a beautiful mosaic from the broken pieces of my life. He restored my tattered heart and turned my ugly mess into precious blessings.

Key:

The psalmist wrote in Psalm 23:3, *"He restores my soul,"* and He does.

Everyone's journey is different. There are no clear-cut directions for healing, but you can invite the Holy Spirit into the process and show yourself grace.

Action Steps:

1. Which part of the story spoke to you? Why?
2. Are you suffering from abandonment issues from any relationship in your past? If so, ask the Holy Spirit to

bring deep healing and position your heart to receive it.

3. Keep a journal and process your healing journey. What is the Holy Spirit speaking to you?

4. Pray, release, and forgive.

5. Be patient with yourself.

13

Daughter of Destiny

*When Jesus had raised Himself up and saw no one but
the woman, He said to her, "Woman, where are those
accusers of yours? Has no one condemned you?"*
(John 8:10 NKJV)

GOD'S GRACE CARRIES us through the hard places.

Raising two active sons as a single mother was
extremely challenging and exhausting. I juggled a full-
time job in the construction industry while attending
recovery meetings and counseling sessions, serving in
church ministry, and taking college courses. I quickly
learned I needed God's grace to survive.

Marrying again was not an option. I was still recuper-
ating from the aftermath of my first marriage. One day
as I read the Bible, my eyes fell on Isaiah 34:16 (NKJV):
*"Search from the book of the Lord and read: Not one of
these shall fail; not one shall lack her mate."*

I laughed, called my girlfriend, who desperately wanted to be married, and shared the verse with her. Surely, this verse was not meant to apply to my life.

The following day, my eyes fell on Isaiah 62:4 (NKJV): *"You shall no longer be termed Forsaken, nor shall your land anymore be termed Desolate; but you shall be called Hephzibah (my delight), and your land Beulah (married); for the Lord delights in you, and your land shall be married."*

I was perplexed and wondering why I kept reading verses on marriage when I was content living a single life, or so I had convinced myself. Finally, I had enough and yelled to heaven, "Fine! I will get married only if You give me a man who worships as David did and loves You with everything in him. He has to be a man who loves me as Christ loves the church and will serve You with all his heart." I argued my case well to stay single, convinced nobody could meet those demands.

God laughed.

I met a guy at church named Michael. Several friends told me that Dr. Mike was the most eligible bachelor in the congregation, but neither of us was interested in a relationship. I had already planned my future and determined I would become a foreign missionary when my sons were old enough.

Michael was tender, kind, and compassionate. We grew close as friends. When we were not together, we spoke for hours on the phone. We had clear-cut boundaries. We prayed and fasted together and talked endlessly about the Lord. I often had visions and saw a double rainbow when we prayed.

My feelings began to intensify toward Michael, and much to my surprise, I started desiring marriage, not necessarily with him, but with whomever the Lord had for me. I assumed the Lord had used this friendship to prepare my heart. I knew Michael was waiting on God for his wife, so I proposed that we pray and fast for each other for a month. He just stared at me and reluctantly agreed.

A month later, while Michael and I were sitting on my couch talking, we kissed. Michael shared that he did not want me to marry anyone else. After faithfully seeking the Lord, we knew God was drawing us together. Michael proposed marriage three months after our conversation, and we were engaged.

Our engagement did not mean smooth sailing. Often plans appointed by the Lord are met with the most significant resistance, and this time was no different. Intense warfare broke out against us. Certain Christians, who felt it was their job to protect Michael from me, weaponized my past to disqualify me as his future wife. They thought they knew better than God what was best for Michael. The accuser of the brethren, working through Christians, attempted to dismantle the healing in my life and shame me back into bondage. Essentially, they were saying that Jesus Christ's blood was insufficient to cleanse my sins and that I was not worthy of God's blessings.

We were in a spiritual battle and fought for our victory in the spiritual realm. Thankfully, we had an army of intercessors who saw the prophetic destiny in our lives and warred for our marriage through prayer. We witnessed the Lord vindicate us from every attack and prepare a table in the presence of our enemies.

"Woman, where are those accusers of yours? Has no one condemned you?"

The attacks on our relationship made us stronger in the Lord. The enemy had meant to tear us apart, but the Lord secured His promise. On our wedding day, there was a double rainbow in the sky, a special kiss from God reminding us of His covenant. He was pouring out His double portion.

Michael and I have now been married for over twenty-three years and have five children—three together and two from my first marriage. We had many difficult times in our marriage and plenty of opportunities to quit, but God remained faithful through every valley. His grace carried us through the hard places.

We co-lead a home church called House Fires and teach others how to hear from God and walk in the gifts of the Holy Spirit. We have seen God move mountains, raise the dead, heal the sick, deliver the addicted, restore broken marriages, and rekindle the backslidden.

God's plans for our lives superseded our limited vision. He not only called me to marriage but also to walk in my rightful identity and authority as His daughter. He called me out of bondage into destiny and wants to do the same for you.

You are God's beautiful one, a daughter of destiny. Today He is calling your name. Rise and heed the voice of God. Your obedience to the Lord will not only impact you but will also impact generations. Don't shrink from the call of God. Don't miss what He wants to accomplish throughout your life. Be open to change.

Key:

When you are about to step into God's destiny, all hell may break loose, but stand firm, knowing that the

One who brought you to it will get you through it. The enemy cannot thwart the plans of God for your life. Set your stake in the ground and refuse to back down to the taunts and accusations of the enemy.

Action Steps:

1. What part of the story spoke most to you? Why do you think that is?
2. Do you believe that the Lord delights in you? In the morning, when you wake, before you allow your mind to wander, remind yourself verbally that God delights in you.
3. Have you been avoiding God in any area of your heart for fear of rejection or pain? If so, take a few moments and offer it to Him. Invite His grace to help you.
4. Has the accuser of the brethren attempted to stop you this season? Pick up your sword and fight!
5. Spend quiet time with the Holy Spirit and ask Him to speak to your heart.

14

Speak Life

Death and life are in the power of the tongue,
and those who love it will eat its fruit.
(Proverbs 18:21 NKJV)

WHAT FRUIT ARE you eating?

I distinctly recall the day a project manager intro-
duced me to a contractor by stating, "Hi, this is Kelly, and
she is the president of the 'man hater's club.'" To say that I
was embarrassed by his introduction was an understate-
ment. At that moment, I wanted to melt into the floor
and disappear. *Why would he say this about me?*

I was horrified that he seemed to believe that about
me enough to state it unflinchingly in an introduction.
His statement had been devoid of humor, so I knew there
were teeth behind the bite, and he wasn't saying it simply
to tease me. *Where did he get the perception that I was a
man-hater?*

The gravity of his statement weighed on my heart. In my prayer time, I asked the Lord about it, and His response was more surprising than the project manager's introduction. The Holy Spirit replied, "Have you ever listened to yourself talk? Start listening."

Taken aback, I tried to be obedient to the Holy Spirit. Over the next few weeks, I intentionally listened to the words that left my mouth and quickly learned why the project manager felt that way. Harsh, sarcastic comments flowed out of my mouth like water, and I realized I was speaking them to conceal the deep-rooted hurt hidden in my heart.

In Matthew 12:34 (NKJV), Jesus says, *"For out of the abundance of the heart the mouth speaks."*

My heart was overflowing with rejection, hurt, and betrayal. Therefore, my mouth responded to the pain as a means of protection. You may often disguise your own hurt and justify your words of death toward yourself or others. This cycle will continue until you find healing in the heart of Jesus.

Unaddressed pain finds a way to draw attention, often in ways that inflict harm to yourself or others. It is your responsibility to heal. You must take every thought captive and control your actions and speech accordingly.

Many years ago, whenever I walked past a mirror, I would cringe at what I saw. I felt so ugly and unworthy. I decreed negative words over myself daily because I believed I was too damaged for anyone to love me. My past trauma was narrating my present thought patterns. Many people had spoken volumes of negative words over my life that took root in my heart's soil.

Words either curse or bless, and the words I spoke over myself were inflicting deep damage. I was a born-again, Spirit-filled Christian, yet I remained held in bondage.

During this season of life, two of my friends and I attended a three-day healing conference. One morning, I confessed to my friends the horrible things I would hear and affirm when I passed a mirror. I told them that even moments before, I had seen my reflection and heard how ugly and unworthy I was. They prayed for me, but what happened next was life changing.

During the morning conference session, I became overwhelmingly tired and confused and had a strong desire just to lie on the floor in complete exhaustion. I could hear the session speaker but could not make out what he was saying. A fog seemed to cover my mind, and I could not concentrate or absorb what was happening. Unbeknownst to me, I was in the middle of warfare, and

God was about to deliver me. Suddenly, with great clarity, I could hear the speaker.

He said, "I will tell you how much Satan does not want you walking in your destiny. Right now, a young woman is sitting in this room who walked by a mirror this morning and heard how ugly and unworthy she is. Every time she passes a mirror, the enemy lies to her. Sister, you are under attack. The enemy wants to keep you from walking in your destiny. Stop listening to the enemy's lies and ask God what He has to say about you."

God had my full attention, and many believers around me began praying for my deliverance. God was setting me free to walk in my purpose and potential. He was purging the words of death from my soul and rewriting a new song of deliverance.

In Job 22:28 (NKJV), we read, *"You will also declare a thing, and it will be established for you; so light will shine on your ways."*

After that profound experience, I began countering the words of death with words of life from the Bible. Every time the enemy tried to speak his lies, I decreed God's truth, and His light began shining on all my ways.

Shortly after the conference, I met my husband, and beyond a doubt, I know I would not be married today had

I not learned to speak life over myself and others. I became who God said I was, and my life dramatically changed.

Key:

You need to speak God's truth over your life to flourish in the freedom of the identity He has made for you. You can walk in freedom and victory today!

Action Steps:

1. After reading the above chapter and Key, can you recognize areas where you have been speaking death instead of life? If so, repent, receive the Lord's forgiveness, and ask the Holy Spirit to bring you in remembrance of His words every time your mouth wants to release death.
2. Ask the Holy Spirit to heal any soul wounds.
3. Be intentional and listen to your words over the next few days. Are you speaking life or death over yourself and others?

Examples:

> I am so _____ (fat, ugly, stupid, dumb, broke, sick).
>
> I will never _____ (have a baby, get married, lose weight, have enough money).
>
> My husband will never change.

4. Stop agreeing with the enemy and start agreeing with God for your life.
5. Make a list of positive daily affirmations to speak over your life.

15

Root Systems

As he thinks in his heart, so is he.
(Proverbs 23:7 NKJV)

WHEN MY HUSBAND and I moved into our first house together, prickly, ugly bushes landscaped the border of the front yard. They were eyesores that prodded and poked painfully if we accidentally rubbed up against them. I am sure they served a purpose, but I didn't like them. I was determined to remove them.

While my husband was away for a neurology conference, I went to Home Depot, rented a rototiller, and bought a shovel and supplies for a large bed of flowers. My goal was to remove those detested bushes and replace them with beautiful flowers to create a new, softer, picturesque view from my window.

Much to my surprise, as I ventured into my project, I encountered massive, gnarly roots so intertwined that it was hard to determine where they originated or ended.

Picking up the most prominent one, I pulled it across my entire yard until I hit the concrete driveway and could not pull further. These heavy roots were thick and entrenched, and I spent significant time chopping them with the shovel. One thing was clear: this job would be more challenging than initially intended. I underestimated the root system that had been in place for many years, and what initially began as a small project turned into an entire weekend of hard work.

Long sweaty hours went by before I completed my goal. The Holy Spirit spoke to me as I labored, turning my project into a spiritual life lesson. He began to show me that many of us have toxic emotions and thought patterns growing in the soil of our hearts. Jealousy, bitterness, unforgiveness, rejection, hatred, and shame are just a few of the emotions that can take root and wreak havoc if left unattended. Over time, they grow so intertwined that they manifest in many areas of our lives without us realizing it. Toxic residue from our wounds leaks, hurting those around us.

Jesus came to set you free, and when you give the Holy Spirit access to every part of your heart without shrinking from the process, He can eradicate those roots that have produced unhealthy and toxic thought patterns. He desires to heal you.

2 Corinthians 10:3–5 (NKJV) tells us, *"For though we walk in the flesh, we do not war according to the flesh. For the weapons of our warfare are not carnal but mighty in God for pulling down strongholds, casting down arguments and every high thing that exalts itself against the knowledge of God, bringing every thought into captivity to the obedience of Christ."*

How you respond to thoughts is vital for spiritual growth and emotional health. Are you carelessly allowing any idea or emotion to take residence in your heart, or are you actively taking them captive to the obedience of Christ? Are you fertilizing and nurturing lies from the pit of hell, or are you aggressively countering that lie with the truth, the Word of God? An unchecked thought system wreaks havoc below the surface of your life.

"Keep your heart with all diligence, for out of it spring the issues of life" Proverbs 4:23 (NKJV).

Do not shrink back when the enemy screams that you are a failure and a loser and when he vomits his condemnation on you. Refuse to allow those lies to take root. Declare the truth that you are a child of God! He has made you fearfully and wonderfully in His image. You are the apple of His eye, and He passionately loves you. Rise in your identity and authority, and remind yourself who you are in Christ! The enemy is under your feet.

Key:

"As we think, we change the physical nature of our brain. As we consciously direct our thinking, we can wire out toxic thinking patterns and replace them with healthy thoughts" (Dr. Caroline Leaf).

Action Steps:

1. Intentionally create a time slot weekly for yourself and God when you won't be distracted. Take your notebook, pen, and Bible, and leave your phone in another room. Ask the Holy Spirit to search your heart and bring to light any places you harbor unproductive, unhealthy roots, for out of those roots grow your thoughts. Once He shows you, ask Him to eradicate them from your heart.

2. This process may require a little fasting and extra prayer. Invite your close prayer partners into the process and ask them to cover you in prayer as you

walk through this step. This action step will help dislodge those roots and bring them to light so you can walk in freedom.

3. Do not walk away with condemnation or unsettling feelings about yourself. If you find yourself experiencing them, it is evidence of one of the roots: self-loathing or shame.

4. Get honest with yourself. What thought patterns have taken root and grown gnarly bushes in your life? Do you recognize bitterness, unforgiveness, comparison, jealousy, or neglect? Don't beat yourself up; get real.

5. Write a letter to God. Tell Him all these thought patterns you have and ask Him to replace them with His thoughts.

Note:

The thoughts don't necessarily fully go away. However, you will recognize them, take authority, and walk in freedom quicker and easier. At first, you may feel exhausted taking every thought captive, but like going to the gym, you will strengthen your muscles each time you put these principles into practice.

16

Living with Purpose

Now therefore, go, and I will be with your mouth
and teach you what you shall say.
(Exodus 4:12 NKJV)

MANY YEARS AGO, I attended a Christian conference, and the speaker asked the crowd of 5,000 people, "Who here knows your God-given purpose?" Approximately 5 percent of the attendees raised their hands. He then asked, "Out of those who raised your hand, who is walking in your purpose?" Maybe 10 percent of those asked raised their hands. Only twenty-five people knew their purpose in a room of 5,000 Christians and were walking in it. That's mind-blowing.

In scripture, Paul compares the body of Christ to our physical bodies, which makes it crucial to understand what our function or purpose is. What would it look like to see 100 percent of Christian believers walking in their calling and making their most significant impact?

We would be an unstoppable force of love advancing the kingdom of God here on earth as it is in heaven.

What if you are part of the 95 percent who do not fully comprehend what God has ordained for your life? How do you discover your purpose? How do you begin to unpack that?

In Ephesians 1:11 (TPT), we read: *"Through our union with Christ, we too have been claimed by God as his own inheritance. Before we were even born, he gave us our destiny; that we would fulfill the plan of God, who always accomplishes every purpose and plan in his heart."*

God knew you before you were born, and He spoke destiny over your life. He intentionally designed you with His divine DNA to accomplish every purpose and plan He ordained. Nobody else can fulfill the calling of God that is on your life. You are uniquely designed to creatively execute His vision for you. Within you are God-sized dreams. Many reading this book are yet-to-be-discovered authors, leaders, musicians, artists, CEOs, pastors, evangelists, NGO directors, and much more.

One of the first things you must do is stop disqualifying yourself based on your ability to accomplish anything. God is your source and strength. You can't limit Him. He is the ultimate Creator, and He does all things well. He did not make a mistake when fashioning you within your mother's womb. "Before we were even born, He gave us our destiny." Amen.

The biblical Moses is an excellent example of this. Moses was a murderer—how could God use him? He was a stutterer—how could he speak? He had been a prince, yet now was a lowly shepherd—was he only fit to lead sheep?

After encountering God in a burning bush and receiving his marching orders, Moses saw himself through a distorted lens. Moses saw his limitations and flaws, while God saw that he would become a deliverer. God is the ultimate Deliverer, yet He called Moses as a conduit, one that He would move through to deliver a nation. He wasn't looking for Moses' skilled resume. He was looking for his *yes*.

After God laid out the plan for Moses to return to Egypt, he gave God every excuse. Why? Moses was looking at his inability, not at God's ability. He saw his weakness, yet God would provide His divine strength.

I imagine God saying," Moses, the enemy tried to kill you while you were a baby, but your momma put you in a basket, and I spared your life. You were supposed to die, but I saved and sustained you before you could even talk.

I've been with you in every situation you've faced because I have marked you. I have sealed you with My purpose from heaven. Moses, this is what we're going to do. I will take you back to Egypt, and you will set my people free."

Moses questioned *God, "How am I going to do that? How on earth am I going to accomplish that? Look at me, God. I am just a shepherd, a man who stutters, a murderer, and one who ran and hid on the backside of the desert. Who am I that you could use me?"*

God tells him, "You got it all wrong, son. It's not who you are but who I AM. You return to Egypt and tell Pharoah that *I AM* is sending you."

I AM the Alpha and Omega.

I AM the Mighty One of Israel.

I AM the Lion of Judah.

I AM the Creator of Heaven and Earth.

I AM the Deliver.

I AM the Healer.

I AM Jehovah Jireh.

I AM Jehovah Shalom.

I AM Jehovah Nissi.

I AM More than Enough.

Boom! Mic drop.

When God asks a question, He already knows the answer. He asked Moses what was in his hands. Moses was carrying a shepherd's rod. God directed Moses to throw his staff down, and in return, He anointed that staff for mighty signs, wonders, and miracles to set the captives free.

When you feel that you don't have what it takes to step through a God-sized door, surrendering what you have to God is vital. If you yield and surrender what is in your hands and heart to God, He will anoint the natural with His supernatural power and give you the ability to walk through the door He is calling you to enter.

God took what was in Moses' hands and fashioned it to deliver an entire nation of slaves. The Holy Spirit is stirring in you and asking, "What is in your hand?"

Are you willing to lay it down to the Lord and open your heart to His plans? He may call you back to Egypt to set the captives free.

2 Corinthians 12:9–10 (ESV): *"But he said to me, 'My grace is sufficient for you, for my power is made perfect in weakness.' Therefore I will boast all the more gladly of my weaknesses, so that the power of Christ may rest upon me. For the sake of Christ, then, I am content with weaknesses, insults, hardships, persecutions, and calamities. For when I am weak, then I am strong."*

The Lord had a plan for Moses' life long before he understood it. Every situation that Moses had been through prepared him, even though he did not immediately recognize it. The same holds true for you. Since you know God gave you destiny and that His Word does not return void, you can rest assured that as you seek Him and ask Him, He will reveal His plan for your life.

Key:

The Lord does not look at your fancy, skilled résumé; He looks for your surrendered heart and your *yes*. You must realize that God wants to reveal Himself to you and wants you to know and understand His plans and purposes.

Action Steps:

- Grab your journal and go to your secret place with the Lord.
- Ask yourself these three questions, and then ask the Holy Spirit:

  1. What dreams do I talk myself out of because they seem too big and impossible?
  2. What am I passionate about? What is in my hand, and what is in my heart?
  3. What could that look like if I surrendered it to God?

God will release strategy from heaven and begin to supernaturally reveal to you His purposes for your life.

17

Personal Vision Statement

Then the Lord answered me and said:
"Write the Vision and make it plain on tablets, that
he may run who reads it. For the vision is yet for an
appointed time; but at the end it will speak, and it will
not lie. Though it tarries, wait for it; because it will surely
come, it will not tarry. Behold the proud, his soul is not
upright in him; but the just shall live by his faith."
(Habakkuk 2:2–4 NKJV)

CLARITY OF VISION is crucial for direction in your life.

If you have ever suffered an eye injury, you understand the injury's impact on your life. Without physical sight, everyday tasks become more challenging to accomplish. Without clarity, everything becomes distorted. If your vision is blocked, you can't see opportunities directly before you.

Recently, I had an eye injury that severely impacted my sight. A hemorrhage clouded my vision, which frustrated me and interrupted my daily life. I could not accomplish my goals without clarity and was limited by the injury until it healed.

You may be walking through life with a spiritual eye injury that hinders your ability to see the God-sized opportunities before you. Creating a vision statement helps to clarify any distortion and navigate beyond the blind spots to accomplish your goals. Once you define your vision, it will be a compass anchoring you to your ultimate *why*.

As a Christian woman, anointed and appointed by God, you want a clear vision that ignites your potential and helps you create your most significant impact while advancing the kingdom of God. This vision should not be burdensome but will bring you joy.

A personal vision statement is a brief, descriptive sentence containing your purpose, passion, and potential. It is a Spirit-directed statement that you write, memorize, and use to keep yourself on track.

I created the following vision statement for myself, leaving room for it to evolve, and I read it daily:

My purpose is to live a healthy, joy-filled, adventurous life with my family, traveling the world, preaching the Gospel, generously giving, and advancing the kingdom of God everywhere I go.

Your statement will be different from mine as you are unique, and so is your God-ordained purpose. My vision statement includes my health, my family, my love to travel, and my purpose to preach God's Word and to give generously to His kingdom. These are blessings that the Lord has declared to my heart.

As you create your vision statement, you can align your daily decisions to support it. For instance, I work with a strength trainer three times a week because health is part of my vision. If an opportunity presents itself that you are unsure of, you can prayerfully consider if it affirms your purpose or distracts from it.

You will identify your passions and potential and create a defining description of what you ultimately desire in the Lord, ensuring it aligns with God's purpose and plan for your life.

Your purpose will support your vision.

Purpose Anchors—Vision Soars

Purpose Clarifies—Vision Ignites

Let's get started. Ask yourself the following questions:

- What currently drives my decisions?
- Are they God- or self-initiated?
- Are they random or intentional?
- Are they prayerful or spontaneous?
- What brings me joy?
- What are my passions?
- What are my core convictions?
- What motivates me?

You will want to prayerfully consider the following four areas:

- Physical: What is your vision for your health? Your body is the temple of the Holy Spirit. The Spirit of God dwells within you.
- Relational: What is your vision for the relationships in your life? God created us to fellowship with one another.

- Spiritual: What is your vision for your spiritual walk? How are you cultivating a healthy spiritual life?

- Emotional: What is your vision for your life? What are your passions? Is it summed up in everyone else's expectations or limitations? Are negative thought patterns limiting your overall belief about your potential?

You may be concerned about putting too much emphasis on yourself and not God. I was guilty of that for a time. I have retrained myself to recognize that I must rise above that chatter to step into my unlimited potential and create my most significant impact. I need to be faithful to pursue the vision that God has revealed in the purpose that He has placed on my life.

Key:

Your personal vision statement will be different from anyone else's because you have unique passions, dreams, and individual God-size assignments. Why do you wake up and work as hard as you do? What are you pursuing? You may not know these answers and may be stuck in a repeat cycle of going through the motions without clear direction.

Action Steps

1. Create your vision statement for the four areas mentioned above (physical, relational, spiritual, and emotional).
2. Look at your answers to the previous question, and create an overall personal vision for your life. Don't limit God, and don't limit yourself. Don't shrink but think BIG. Think God-sized dreams and visions. Create one overall vision statement for yourself. Why do you want to grow? Dig deep and challenge yourself. Don't look at your past mistakes or limitations, but focus on the God-size potential inside of you.
3. Create five to ten life commandments or personal convictions to help you walk in your vision. Print them out, and read them every morning and night.

18

Burn the Boat

And Peter answered Him and said, "Lord, if it is You,
command me to come to You on the water." So He said,
"Come." And when Peter had come down out of the boat,
he walked on the water to go to Jesus.
(Matthew 14:28–29 NKJV)

A BOAT BOBS in the middle of the sea, shrouded by the darkness of the night. Wildly tossed to and fro by relentless winds, the vessel falters. Terror grips the disciples in the boat. Suddenly, Jesus appears as if an apparition, walking on the turbulent water. The disciples cower in fear, believing that He must be a ghost. But Jesus immediately calms them, saying, "Be of good cheer! It is I; do not be afraid."

Calling to Jesus, Peter bravely steps out in faith to walk to Him. With his eyes firmly on Jesus, he also walks on water, forgetting the fear of the raging storm around them. He falters when his faith fails—when he looks at the storm instead of the miraculous power of the God he serves. Catching him, Jesus helps him into the boat, and the storm stills. Passion pushed Peter into the waves, but without faith in the power of his God-given purpose, he stumbles and sinks.

I was unfamiliar with human trafficking when someone from church invited me to volunteer at an event that presented the topic in Philadelphia. Little did I know that the seeds planted that day would blossom into a powerful ministry in the future.

A friend of mine, Carol Gleeson, was a full-time missionary in Guatemala with her organization Operation Jabez. She shared stories about women who prostituted themselves to feed their children. Carol started a sewing school in her home, and with permission from the pimps, she invited the women to attend classes. She taught the women to sew, gave them sewing machines, and helped them create micro-businesses that they could learn to leverage successfully. Instead of selling their bodies, these precious women could sell merchandise in the local market to tourists. Carol was restoring their dignity.

I had a restless tension welling inside of me. I deeply desired to make a significant spiritual impact like Carol, but I felt tethered to my everyday responsibilities at home. Hearing her stories stirred my soul and propelled me into a season of deep prayer and seeking God. I sensed a stirring in me for God's purpose that was too great to ignore. My soul was contending for the promises spoken over my life, and I cried day and night in prayer. I wanted my life to make a significant difference and wanted to walk on water like Peter. Yet somehow I wondered if I was qualified for a God-sized vision.

One night while driving to a strategic prayer gathering in New Jersey, my husband and I stopped at a local coffee shop. When I stepped through the front door, I saw the back of a man's head, his body poorly shielding his laptop screen. I was shocked when I inadvertently saw what he was watching. To my horror, the screen exposed a pubescent boy in a sexual position with a grown man. I was stunned and sickened, taken off guard by what I saw. The man seemed to show no shame in consuming this in public.

My brain tried to process the scene; my mind started playing tricks on me in a dance of cognitive dissonance. I tried to rationalize the situation mentally: *What if it was just two consenting adults on the screen? Porn is not illegal. Maybe it wasn't a child being sexually abused and exploited. I had seen it only briefly, and perhaps I was mistaken.* My heart knew the truth and grew heavy. As I exited the coffee shop, I took a long hard look at the man's face to obtain a good description for the police.

Once in my car, I immediately contacted the local police and described what had happened. I decided if I were going to err, I would err on the side of protecting a child. What if that porn was a live feed and a child was in danger? After the police went to the coffee shop, they called me back and informed me that the employee denied anyone being in the store on a computer. Why would that employee lie unless he was covering for something illegal? My heart hurt for the innocent child.

While my heart weighed what I had witnessed, the Lord was commissioning me for His calling. Later, I dreamt of looking down into a room filled with ladies and young girls. They did not see me, but I had a bird's eye view. A young girl was lying down on a beautiful ornate chair. No words were spoken, but I knew someone had sexually abused her and the others and that I needed to help them. When I awoke, it was unlike any previous dream. I felt that God was commissioning me to minister to the sexually exploited.

Not much seemed to change in my life. I was still taking care of my children, tending the house, and performing my ordinary daily routine. God dug up the fallow ground in my heart and prepared me for His plans and purposes through this season. Each day I held up the prophetic words that had been spoken over my life and surrendered to His intents and purposes, even before knowing what they were. The word *yes* became my daily prayer. *Yes*, God, I will go where You tell me to go. *Yes*, God, I will speak what You tell me to speak. *Yes*, God, I will do what You ask me to do.

The Holy Spirit spoke.

A couple of months later, I was doing my laundry and heard these words in my spirit: "Start a breakfast and call it 'Dining for Dignity.'" A holy download of God's whispers started pouring into me, and I realized the Holy Spirit gave me direction. It was as if He were saying, "You have the opportunity to gather together in this nation freely and dine, and in doing so, restore dignity to victims of sexual exploitation." Although I did not fully comprehend the direction and vision at the moment, I knew that God was steering me.

This breakfast meeting could be an opportunity to shine a light on Carol Gleeson's ministry and a place to sell the hand-sewn items from the ladies in Guatemala. Nevertheless, I knew this was not only about Operation Jabez. Many blank spaces were yet to be filled, but I knew the Holy Spirit spoke to me, and His work was underway.

As I pondered this new direction, I took my eyes off the Lord and put them on myself. I began to wonder what others would think. Like Peter, who took his eyes off the Lord, I began to sink.

Why would I start a breakfast meeting? That's ridiculous. Why should I call it Dining for Dignity? People are going to think I am weird. Who would come? What would people think? Then I began bartering with the Lord. *How about I just have breakfast, not make too much noise, and certainly not give it a title?* I was already talking myself out of God's direction. I called my friend Irene to see what she thought. "Clearly, this is God, Kelly; you need to do this," she responded. I called another friend, and she laughed and confirmed it was God.

When God called me to step out of the boat, I did not realize the magnitude of that seemingly small direction from the Holy Spirit and how obeying would catapult me into a life-changing journey. He called me out of the boat to join Him in unexplored waters.

I took a step of faith and set the plans for the breakfast. This season of my life was like jumping out of an airplane and hoping I had a parachute.

And so it began.

The first Dining for Dignity breakfast was held in July 2011 at a country club in New Jersey. Many women attended, and it was clear that God was opening the door and paving the way for a unique ministry. Although I highlighted Operation Jabez from Guatemala and sold the handmade items, it was undeniable that God was calling me into something more.

Knowing I would share about prostitution in Guatemala, I began researching the topic. I read the first article about a teen girl in Central America who sold her virginity to an American businessman for $4.50. Glued to my computer, I read story after story of international sex trafficking. I could not wrap my mind around the reality that young women and children were sold as commodities worldwide.

Late one night, as I scrolled through Amazon, I stumbled upon a book called *God in a Brothel*. On the front cover was a picture of a young girl lying on a beautiful ornate chair, and I knew that was the same girl and room I had seen in my earlier dream. I was consumed with a holy fire to make a difference. God was putting the pieces together.

God gave me a choice. Would I use my voice, passion, and platform to make a difference, or would I ignore the call that the Holy Spirit had placed on my heart? I could go back to life as usual, pretending I did not know about human trafficking and sex tourism, or I could sound the clarion call and join the battle.

As I sat crying in my dining room, something supernatural ignited in my heart. There was righteous indignation within me. Ignorance was no longer an option after the Lord had revealed this dark evil to me.

The Dining for Dignity breakfast quickly turned the corner from a sweet time of fellowship and selling handmade items to a battle cry to expose human sex trafficking. Each meeting built upon the last, and more and more people heard about our group. I intentionally invited men to recognize their essential role in fighting sexual exploitation. The momentum was growing and taking on a force bigger than us. It was clear that I was rallying the troops. My mission was to raise awareness, provoke people to action, and create change.

My next logical step was to become a legal non-profit to maximize the reach of our influence. My husband

and I financed all the operating costs for the first year. While researching non-profits, I read several articles that posed the following question: "Is it necessary to start a new organization if someone else is already doing it?" I found dozens of organizations raising awareness about human trafficking and sexual exploitation. Doubt entered in, and I began to question whether to proceed. *Perhaps I didn't hear from God?* Unfettered by my doubt, the Lord kept driving this vision while opening doors to form a non-profit and a tax-exempt 501(c)(3) with a wider sphere of influence.

Those words spoken to me to start a breakfast called Dining for Dignity proved to be a valuable lesson. Soon after filing for our business, I discovered that Dining for Dignity was available for us; but Dining with Dignity was already taken by another organization. That small three-letter word "for" was vital. God showed me that He would speak and lead, and I needed to listen for the small details.

Although the topic of human trafficking is heavy, the Lord gave me supernatural grace to stand and press forward. We made a massive impact as an organization, and community leaders and the media recognized our efforts and considered me an expert in the field. I spoke on television, radio, and podcasts, and I was interviewed for newspapers.

Who knew that a small act of obedience could activate such a response? God did. We can't put God in a box. We need to be willing to explore the possibilities, the God-sized dreams He has for us, even when they don't make sense.

The Lord does not call the qualified, but He qualifies the called. A bold step of faith can be used to guide a generation to freedom.

Philippians 4:13 (NKJV) promises, *"I can do all things through Christ who strengthens me."*

God can do whatever He wants with whomever He chooses. He does not need our fancy résumés but only our yielded hearts. God called unqualified men and women to perform great exploits throughout the Bible, and He still calls them today.

Key:

Peter did not walk on water; he walked on the Word of God. When you operate in the spiritual realm, obeying God's voice instead of your limitations, you will witness supernatural miracles in your midst.

Action Steps:

1. What are your godly passions?

2. What are the limitations that prevent you from trusting God? Peter chose to look beyond the physical limits of the storm and boat and step out into the limitless possibilities with God.

3. Offer your doubts and fears to God and ask for the courage to believe Him.

4. I almost talked myself out of starting the breakfast because of a man-fearing, man-pleasing spirit. Identify where you allow a man-fearing spirit and ask God to help you overcome that.

5. What could you accomplish if nothing were stopping you? Pray boldly, asking God to open the doors of possibilities for you.

19

Identity Theft

The thief does not come except to steal, and to kill,
and to destroy. I have come that they may have life,
and that they may have it more abundantly.
(John 10:10 NKJV)

EXCITED TO MEET my husband at a coffee shop for a midday mini-date, I hurried in to find a table a few minutes early. People were scattered throughout the café munching on muffins and drinking their lattes in busy little conversation circles. Fueled by caffeine and the anticipation of sharing the thoughts stirring in my heart, I immediately entered an enthusiastic conversation with my husband when he arrived. I was eager to share all the details about a bold mission trip I had just returned from the previous night.

No one was more surprised than I was when the team of XXX Church, a Christian organization, invited me on a mission trip to a New Jersey pornography convention to share the Gospel with thousands of people. While others attended to pursue their sexual fantasies, I was part of a Christian ministry team that handed out Bibles and prayed with people. This mission trip was not an ordinary adventure—and not one most Christians would engage in or understand.

Throughout the weekend, God wrecked my comfortable Christianity and gave me a supernatural ability to love His children. What I witnessed was overwhelming. My heart broke as I witnessed young girls being leered at by lascivious onlookers as they posed suggestively on display for the sex-hungry masses. As a mother, all I could think about was that each of these girls was someone's daughter. They were precious, created in the image of God, yet they were in the clutches of the enemy's grip.

We ministered by shining our lights in a place shadowed in darkness. As Christians, though we are careful to walk with wisdom, we do not need to fear the dark, nor should we hide from it. The light of Christ illuminates the darkness and draws people to God.

Here's another way to put it: You're here to be light, bringing out the God-colors in the world. God is not a secret to be kept. We're going public with this, as public as

a city on a hill. If I make you light-bearers,
you don't think I'm going to hide you under a bucket,
do you? I'm putting you on a light stand. Now that I've
put you there on a hilltop, on a light stand—shine!
Keep open house; be generous with your lives. By opening
up to others, you'll prompt people to open up with God,
this generous Father in heaven.
(Matthew 5:14–16 MSG)

As I recounted my experience to my husband while sitting in the Starbucks, a woman positioned in the seat behind me forcibly bumped my chair. She apologized and explained that she was reaching for her purse. But I immediately saw her bag resting on the other side. Feeling unsettled, I grabbed my pocketbook from the back of my chair and placed it on the table in front of me. It was too late.

This woman had stolen my identification and all my credit cards. When I arrived home, messages from various fraud departments were already waiting for me. The thief had racked up thousands of dollars of charges in just an hour.

Waves of anger, concern, and powerlessness swept over me as I dealt with the hours of frustrating follow-up, knowing that a stranger held my identity in her possession.

The violation shook me. As my husband and I walked through the journey of restoring our accounts and all kinds of problematic security issues, I began to see that God was guiding me through what would become the heart of the next season of my life and calling.

My emotions were raw, and I hit the pause button to walk around my neighborhood park to clear my head and hear from God. The Holy Spirit asked me, "Kelly, why are you so upset, and what is your fear?"

Immediately I responded and said, "Identity theft."

At that moment, the Holy Spirit spoke clearly to my heart and gave me words to describe what I experienced at the pornography convention. He whispered, "Kelly, that is what you witnessed this past weekend. The women you met at Exxxotica are victims of identity theft in the foulest form. The enemy, the thief, has stolen their identity as daughters of God; now, you go out and tell My daughters who they are."

These were not merely words from the Holy Spirit but a supernatural calling and commissioning sealed within my heart to reach women working in the sex industry.

God spoke to me, "Kelly, are you willing to be a light in the darkness? It is easy to curse the dark, but are you willing to be a light? Will you walk like Jesus, showing the most oppressed that they are beautiful treasures? Will you rescue those on the brink of death by showing them that there is always hope and that it is never too late? They can have their identity restored by the power of Jesus Christ. These women hold intrinsic value, but they don't know it. They are treasures in the darkness. Will you go tell them?"

When God is weaving a new season in your life, you never know what threads He will use. He is full of surprises and will often redirect your path, catapulting you into exciting new adventures. Little did I know my mission trip to a pornography convention, coupled with someone stealing my credit cards, would lead me into a cutting-edge ministry helping the sexually exploited discover their authentic identity.

Key:

All our callings are different. Don't get caught up in comparison. Stay in your lane, for that's where the anointing will be for you.

Action Steps:

1. Ask the Holy Spirit what your mission is and to direct you.
2. Don't be afraid of stepping outside your comfort zone.
3. Give God your *yes*.
4. Pray with an open heart and anticipation that your God, the Creator of the universe, has a divine purpose for you.
5. Make yourself available to God and allow Him to inconvenience you. In those times of inconvenience, you often find great rewards with God.

20

A Song of Destiny

Adonai your God is in your midst—a mighty Savior! He
will delight over you with joy. He will quiet you with His
love. He will dance for joy over you with singing.
(Zephaniah 3:17 TLV)

WORDS ARE POWERFUL.

Music has a uniquely compelling way of impacting
our emotions. Often, the words and melody of a beautiful worship song flow through my heart and mind at
various times of the day. Sometimes I wake up singing a
song I have not heard in twenty years, but the words are
still tucked deep within me and give me strength and joy
for the day.

Contrasting the joy and peace that praise music
provides, when I minister inside strip clubs, the music
blares so loudly it pierces the atmosphere with degrading
lyrics toward women. The beat's intensity and repetitive
vulgar lyrics create a hostile environment, disrespecting

the dancers, reducing them to sex objects, and labeling them with expletives. The price tag of dancing in a strip club is much higher than they could know because the words enter not only the ears of the listeners but also their very hearts and souls.

You probably have not worked in a strip club, but you may have been subject to foul, degrading lyrics on repeat, and you may still carry the hurtful, mean words that others have spoken into your life. Deep in the cavern of your heart are hidden pains caused by others' careless words. The hidden damage has influenced how you present your authentic self to the world.

You may have had people in your life release a negative sound of disgrace and shame over you since birth, creating a sense of unworthiness. Instead of declaring a destiny filled with purpose and potential, those voices prophesied failure and rejection. As an adult, you have learned to put on the business suit, lipstick, and heels, but you cannot seem to break the lies binding your heart and limiting your potential.

The good news is that your perspective can change today. Other people's inability to see your worth and their attempt to imprison you with their words are not a reflection of truth.

Destiny awaits.

The Lord sings another song over you, breaking the chains, destroying the bondage of every lie spoken into your heart. Scripture says that God rejoices over you with singing. The words He sings are life and freedom. He releases a melody of love with a rhythm of joy, fully embracing you as His daughter. The enemy tries to devalue and destroy you, but God breaks every chain. Instead of seeing your shortcomings, He sees a reflection of Himself in your life.

I heard a story—a beautiful fiction woven as lore that, real or not, stirs the heart. It tells a moving story of a woman who, upon discovering that she is pregnant, goes alone into the wilderness and waits until she receives a song of destiny for her unborn baby. Once she receives that song, she returns to teach the words and melody to everyone in her community. When the time for the birth draws near, the woman is surrounded by gatherers who sing the song of destiny while she labors. This song of destiny covers the baby in a uniquely enchanting sound only created for her. She is born enveloped in destiny. The song calls to her, carrying its meaningful melody over her life. As the child grows, this song is sung on every momentous milestone occasion in her life, reminding the child of her destiny.

As the child grows, she isn't met with scorn or derision if she makes poor or destructive decisions. Instead, she is met with a caring community singing her song. She is surrounded by a circle of people singing love, truth, and destiny over her life. This reminder of who she is brings hope instead of humiliation or condemnation. The released sound of hope, a song of destiny, allows the prophetic words of possibility and potential to pierce the shame and break the lies.

Can you imagine how powerful that must be? For one moment, picture yourself in your exposed sin, every eye looking your way. You are waiting for the judgment to come down against you. You are anticipating and rehearsing the words of shame they will release. However, you hear a sound of forgiveness and destiny instead of condemnation. Grace instead of shame is your portion, says the Lord.

God is the only one in the entire universe who knows you in full disclosure and still loves you. No one knows every detail, flaw, or strength about your life except God, yet He delights in you and rejoices over you with singing. His song is a song of destiny.

Key:

Words spoken by others do not define you, only those spoken by God.

Action Steps:

1. Get alone with God and worship Him for a few minutes to align your spirit with His. Then ask the Holy Spirit to search your heart for unhealed wounds caused by harmful words spoken over you.

2. Draw a line down the center of a piece of paper and write out every lie spoken over you on one side, which the Holy Spirit brings into remembrance. Then counter that lie with words of truth that God says about you on the opposite side.

3. Bring your emotions and thoughts into alignment with the truth. Reject the lies.

4. Choose to forgive those people who spoke those lies over you. Speak a blessing over them.

5. If you find these steps are too deep for you to handle alone, bring a trusted prayer partner into the process. Don't dig; allow the Holy Spirit to uncover. He will

give you the grace to walk through the emotions and healing as He reveals.

6. Visit these action steps often. Healing is not a one-and-done situation. Be patient with God and yourself, and be open to His process.

21

Elohim

But He needed to go through Samaria.

(John 4:4 NKJV)

THE GOLDEN RAYS of the rising Mississippi sun glinted through my fifth-floor hotel window as I silently sipped tea, the warm mug clutched tightly in my hands. Steam rose then dissipated as I sighed on an exhale, steeling myself mentally for my last day of prison ministry. *What would this day of ministry bring?* I quietly wondered as I allowed the Holy Spirit to refuel my heart and mind.

As I sat sipping, I delighted in images of beautiful testimonies from the week replaying in my mind. Serving within the walls of prison ministry, I had the immense privilege of seeing the power of God on full display as He set captives free in His great grace and power. As I rested in these thoughts, marveling at what the Lord continued to do, the Holy Spirit interrupted my reveling to ask a question: "Do you trust Me?" the Holy Spirit questioned.

"Yes, of course, I trust You, Lord. That's why I am here," I responded matter-of-factly.

A sweet chuckle, a heavenly laugh, echoed inside me as if the Father Himself was delighted in my response. "Good; it will be exhilarating," I heard the Holy Spirit tell me.

Instantly, an open vision filled my mind in which I was riding on the back of a Harley-Davidson motorcycle. A large man wearing a leather jacket and a biker's helmet sat in front of me as I tightly gripped his waist. The wind whipped at our hair as we sped down the highway—my unruly red mane dancing behind me, cascading around me in the oncoming air currents. Awash in delight, we sped forward, excitement and joy infiltrating my heart and filling me with great expectations.

Knock! Knock! Knock!

I was jolted from my reverie by a fist pounding on my hotel room door.

Opening the door, I greeted my partners in ministry, Tammy and Jodi, who had traveled with me from New Jersey to serve in the prisons. They had arrived at my hotel room to pray with me before the upcoming day of ministry. I shared the vision and the word from the Lord with them. We assumed the spiritual encounter pertained to our scheduled visit to the men's section that morning and prayed into it. We were unsure of what to expect, but we were eager to see the Holy Spirit work.

The Uber driver dropped us off at the main prison building where the superintendent was waiting. He informed us there had been a gang-related fight in the men's building earlier that the morning, and we could no longer visit there. The entire building was on lock-down. Instead, we would hold a morning presentation with the ladies, followed by visitations to Pods A, B, and C, the buildings where the ladies slept. Friday was a day off from mandatory work, and most of the ladies would be at the pods.

The warden escorted us through security at each building, where two armed guards sat in an elevated station with bulletproof glass, surveying the surroundings. The facility carried an air of intimidation with high open ceilings contrasting the cold, hard exposed concrete floors, which funneled into one main open area. Scattered metal picnic tables welded to the floor and a lone television mounted on the wall created a starkly crude gathering place. A group of women scattered haphazardly on sturdy metal benches stared aimlessly at the tabloid show blaring on the television. Five or six hallways lined with beds on both sides of the corridor extended from the main room, reminding me of spokes on a wheel. Ladies gathered in clusters at the tables and beds, talking or playing cards. Many women recognized me, stopped what they were doing, and came over to say hello.

Because there were nearly 200 ladies in each building, we trusted the Holy Spirit to highlight who we needed to pray with and what to say. The response to our visit was terrific. The women were happy to see us, and God's presence was evident. His joy and love poured through those rooms, infusing His daughters with hope. My heart leapt at the encouragement.

As the end of the day neared, we had one last pod to visit. We walked past security, visually scouring the room for those the Lord would highlight. I was chatting with a group of women at a table when a young lady caught my eye. She was standing by herself, observing us. She had a turban on her head bearing the word *Elohim,* a Hebrew word for God that also translates to "strength and might." I approached her and asked if I could pray. She silently nodded her head *yes.* Vivacious and exuberant, I naturally speak at an elevated volume, my voice carrying over others. Given the constant clamor of the crowd and the hum and buzz of conversations around me, I spoke even more assertively and loudly in this environment. However, as I began to talk to this woman, the Holy Spirit nudged me to speak in a gentle, soft-sounding voice, and I obeyed.

"What is your name?" I prompted tenderly.

The woman replied that her name was Davina. I looked her in the eyes and said, "Davina, the Holy Spirit is not the author of your pain. The Holy Spirit is not the author of your trauma." She gazed at me, gaping, and did not say a word.

I continued, "Davina, the Holy Spirit is the author of your healing and deliverance." No response, only an unnerving stare.

"Davina, just because nobody showed you love while growing up does not mean you are not loveable. Just because nobody valued you does not mean you are not valuable." Tears started streaming down her face in response to my words.

I continued, "Davina, I am going to pray for you. Is it okay if I touch your shoulder?" She nodded her head *yes*.

I lightly touched her right shoulder and said, "In the name of Jesus." She instantly stiffened, falling straight back as she plunged head-first toward the concrete floor. I lunged and caught her before she hit the concrete. Her body became startlingly ramrod straight, and she appeared to start levitating off the floor. She began writhing—curving like a snake from her hips up, yet her lower body was still board stiff. Her head and eyes rolled back, and she growled out a roar from the pit of hell. My heart started racing, and then I heard the Holy Spirit whisper: "I told you it would be exhilarating." My shock turned to excitement as I knew God had prepared me and He was about to deliver His daughter, Davina.

I did not want to draw any more attention to us, so I leaned against the wall to hide Davina's view from the armed security guards and started praying for deliverance in the name of Jesus. She moved unnaturally, her body surging up and down, erupting in disconcerting unworldly sounds as I took authority in the name of Jesus. Other inmates realized what was happening and joined me in prayer, circling Davina.

After a minute or two, Davina was silent and peacefully still. I sat waiting for her to wake to explain that Jesus had set her free. Before I had the opportunity, Tammy tapped me on the shoulder, saying the warden wanted us to leave immediately. As we walked out of the room, we overheard ladies reporting that demons plagued Davina nightly, turning silent sleep into tortured screams.

When we returned to the warden's car, I discovered that she hadn't removed us because she was upset with us—she simply needed to leave as her shift had ended. As we drove back to the main building, I reflected on John 4 in the Bible. Scripture tells us that Jesus needed to go the way of Samaria. He was on a mission to encounter the woman at the well and set her free. I realized that Jesus needed to go the way of central Mississippi to encounter a young lady named Davina, where He radically set her free.

And these signs will follow those who believe:
In My name, they will cast out demons.
(Mark 16:17 NKJV)

Key:

God did not need me, but He invited me into a beautiful and exciting work of deliverance.

Action Steps:

1. Read Mark 16:14–18. Are there any portions you have not believed? Ask God to remove any fear and to stretch your faith.
2. Ask God for opportunities to pray for others.
3. Make yourself available to the Lord. Don't be so busy that you miss your opportunities.

22

A Divine Rendezvous

A man's heart plans his way,
but the Lord directs his steps.
(Proverbs 16:9 NKJV)

WETUMPKA, ALABAMA, WAS never on my bucket list of places to visit. In fact, I had never even heard of the city until I received a call from Chaplain Bradford from Tutwiler prison located in Wetumpka. This city wasn't on my radar, yet God called me to minister there.

Chaplain Bradford was preparing Christmas gift bags for 800 female inmates and asked if I would donate copies of my book, *SHINE: Uplifting Words for Girls in Stilettos*, and I did. The ladies responded so well to *SHINE* that the chaplain invited me as their guest speaker over Mother's Day weekend. Excitedly, I agreed. Unknown to me, the chaplain's invitation was a doorway to a divine setup. The Lord was inviting me into a rendezvous with grief and healing. He just hadn't revealed it yet.

The chaplain reported that inmates buzzed excitedly about my visit, and there was a waiting list for the scheduled chapel services where I was assigned to speak. I was looking forward to sharing the freedom I found in Jesus with these women.

Since I rarely ministered alone, Tammy, my ministry partner, planned to join me on the trip to Wetumpka. We spent weeks planning the trip and looked forward to visiting Tutwiler for the first time. Our itinerary included flying to Mobile, Alabama, and driving three hours to Wetumpka. There we would spend two days of ministry before returning to Mobile.

The chaplain from Mobile Metro Jail wanted to meet me since I had been sending copies of *SHINE* for several years. Due to COVID regulations and protocol, I would not be able to speak to the inmates but was invited to visit and tour the facility.

Two days before our scheduled travel, Tammy tested positive for COVID and was kept sick in bed. At that moment, all of our plans were interrupted, and the Lord redirected my steps. After much prayer and discussion, I postponed the Tutwiler prison ministry until Tammy could join me. We had collectively put much effort into this trip, and now I had to cancel at the last minute. I felt terrible for disappointing the chaplain and inmates.

Since I had a paid, non-refundable airline ticket and was familiar with the area, I still flew to Mobile. My mother had lived there for nearly thirty years, so everything about the city reminded me of her. My mom had passed away the year before, and I was flying in on her birthday. It was no accident that God shifted my plans and placed me there on that specific day, wrapped in my mother's memories.

My original schedule would have distracted me from the memories and emotions that washed over me, but the Lord shifted those plans. He removed the distractions so He could have my full attention. God was not after my ministry. He was after my heart.

I tried my best to prepare as the plane landed, reminding myself that my mom would not be greeting me as I exited the airport doors. Ever since my mother died, I have wrestled with two questions that lay heavy on my heart: *Why did my mom have to suffer so much in life?* and *Why did she suffer so much while dying?* I couldn't understand why God allowed her to endure such pain.

I spent Mother's Day alone, reflecting and reading poolside at the hotel. The Alabama sun was hot, but the clear skies and shade from the trees presented a tempo-rary oasis for me. I knew the Holy Spirit wanted to do business with my heart, and He was patiently waiting for me. As I turned a page in the book I was reading, my eyes fell on one sentence: "God is just, and He can't be unjust." I reread it and spoke the sentence out loud.

As if someone had taken a key and unlocked my heart, I immediately sensed freedom and understanding for the questions I had been asking. I looked upward and repented to God for questioning His goodness. Yes, my mother suffered, but that did not mean God was unjust. The Holy Spirit swept me up into a heavenly encounter. The green trees looked the brightest green I had ever seen. The blue sky seemed brilliant, more colorful than ever. A supernatural peace flooded my soul, and the Father's love enveloped me, reminding me of His goodness. He was healing my heart, and I didn't want this precious time to end. I savored this feeling, knowing that God was working all things together in His unfathomable love and mercy for my good and His glory.

After several minutes, I sensed the Holy Spirit prompting me to go upstairs, where I knew I would have a message. I returned to my hotel room to find an email and voicemail from the chaplain's office at the county jail. They confirmed my visit for the following day and announced that I had permission to speak with the inmates. My heart was bursting with joy. I had been trying to obtain permission to talk to the Mobile inmates since 2018, and in one moment, the Lord redirected my steps and opened the previously shut doors.

Just minutes prior, the Lord had set my heart free, and now He was calling me to the jail so He could set the captives free. I planned on speaking at Julia Tutwiler prison, but God shut that door and opened the door for me at Mobile Metro Jail.

His ways are higher than ours. God unleashed His Spirit and ignited Mobile Metro jail the following day. Spontaneous worship broke out, and inmates, chaplains, and the captain of the guards had their arms in the air worshipping the Lord, with tears streaming down their faces.

The Holy Spirit deposited supernatural hope. Women experienced more freedom behind bars than they ever had on the streets. Not only did He bless the inmates, but He also poured out His Spirit on the guards and employees. There was a tangible joy that was not there when I arrived. God set hearts free!

The captain of the guards, chaplains, and I worshipped and prayed our way back to their office. We were experiencing a profound move of God and basked in His presence.

When I returned home to New Jersey, the chaplain sent me a message: "Ms. Master, we are still experiencing the rippling effects of your powerful ministry. What a lasting encounter this jail experienced. Will you consider holding weekly Bible studies via Zoom with the ladies?"

God had divinely orchestrated the entire trip. He knew Tammy would get COVID, and He supernaturally directed my steps, opened doors that I could not open myself, and poured out His presence on many. He healed my heart and then poured Himself through it. What initially looked like a setback was a setup for a divine rendezvous with significant impact.

Now the Lord is the Spirit,
and where the Spirit of the Lord is, there is freedom.
(2 Corinthians 3:17 ESV)

Key:

The Holy Spirit is always working. He brings hope and healing, ministering to ALL of his children. A closed door is not a sign of discouragement; instead, it is divine encouragement that God is opening a new door and direction.

Action Steps:

1. Pray and ask the Lord to guide your steps in all things.
2. Trust Him to lead you where He wants you to go, opening divine doors that were previously closed.
3. Praise Him for the work that He will do in your life.
4. Ask Him to allow you to serve wherever He places you, giving Him praise in all circumstances.

23

The Commissioning

Forget about what's happened; don't keep going
over old history. Be alert, be present. I'm about to do
something brand-new. It's bursting out! Don't you see it?
There it is! I'm making a road through the desert,
rivers in the badlands.
(Isaiah 43:18–19 MSG)

SISTER, YOU STAND at the threshold of a wild and wonderful adventure with God. Dream big. Permit yourself to soar to new heights and explore realms of possibilities with Him. He has increased your spiritual vision and stretched your faith. He is about to do something brand new in your life, and it's bursting out. Don't you see it?

Lay hold of your prophetic destiny with tenacity and grit. Refuse to back down in the face of unjust accusations! You are no longer bound by a man-fearing spirit. You don't need man's approval to operate in your calling; you have God's endorsement.

All limits are off. There is no red tape with God. Take a bold leap of faith! It is time to step out of the old and into the new and soar with an untethered vision—no more playing it safe. Get off the sidelines, and emerge from the shadows. You were born to shine!

You are free.

You are enough.

You are worthy.

You are an overcomer.

You are a woman of impact.

You are a daughter of God.

You are a world changer.

Embrace all the Holy Spirit has done on this *Fierce and Free* journey, knowing it's not over but just beginning.

Rise, O woman of God, pick up your sword, and fight! Put your stake in the ground, draw a line of demarcation, and release a clarion call to all of heaven and hell. You are a daughter of the Almighty God who walks in covenant promises. His Word cannot and will not return void in your life. When God works, no man can reverse it.

God has called you forth for such a time as this. His eyes are upon you, and you are never alone. There is a strong anointing upon your life. Come into agreement with the promises of God. Command forth the gifts and callings.

Your past does not dictate your future. Break every generational curse and familiar spirit assigned to your bloodline and walk in identity and authority. Go deeper with intercession and communion. You have the mind of Christ, and no weapon formed against you shall prosper. Shift spiritual atmospheres. Crush the works of darkness and advance the kingdom of light, for you are seated in heavenly places.

Father God, I come before Your throne of grace and mercy, in the mighty name of Jesus, standing in the gap for my sister. I pray that You elevate her thinking and expand her influence and impact. Lord, shut the doors that need to be closed and open the doors that need to be open. Release supernatural creativity, strategy, and wisdom. I declare the blood of Jesus over her destiny. Lord, I pray that You will increase my sister's faith and anoint her with supernatural boldness to live fierce and free!

CPSIA information can be obtained
at www.ICGtesting.com
Printed in the USA
BVHW032221240123
657059BV00003B/185

9 781956 267990